Oracle Dat~
Data Mo~
Schema D~ ~n for
JSON-Relational
Duality

Beda Hammerschmidt

Pascal Desmarets

Steve Hoberman

Align > Refine > Design
Series

Technics Publications

Published by:

115 Linda Vista, Sedona, AZ 86336 USA
https://www.TechnicsPub.com

Edited by Sadie Hoberman
Cover design by Lorena Molinari

First Printing 2024
Copyright © 2024 by Technics Publications

ISBN, print ed.	9781634623636
ISBN, Kindle ed.	9781634623643
ISBN, ePub ed.	9781634623674
ISBN, PDF ed.	9781634623681

Library of Congress Control Number: 2023934017

Contents

Figures

Tables

About the Book

My daughter can make a mean brownie. She starts with a store-bought brownie mix and adds chocolate chips, apple cider vinegar, and other "secret" ingredients to make her own unique delicious brownie.

Building a robust database design meeting users' needs requires a similar approach. The store-bought brownie mix represents a proven recipe for success. Likewise, there are data modeling practices that have proven successful over many decades. The chocolate chips and other secret ingredients represent the special additions that lead to an exceptional product. Oracle duality views have a number of special design considerations, much like the chocolate chips. Combining proven data modeling practices with Oracle duality views design-specific practices creates a series of data models representing powerful communication tools, greatly improving the opportunities for an exceptional design and application.

In fact, each book in the Align > Refine > Design series covers conceptual, logical, and physical data modeling for a specific database product, combining the best of data modeling practices with solution-specific design considerations. It is a winning combination.

My daughter's first few brownies were not a success, although as the proud (and hungry) dad, I ate them anyway—and they were still pretty tasty. It took practice to get the brownie to come out amazing. We need practice on the modeling side as well. Therefore, each book in the series follows the same animal shelter case study, allowing you to see the modeling techniques applied to reinforce your learning.

If you want to learn how to build multiple database solutions, read all the books in the series. Once you read one, you can pick up the techniques for another database solution even quicker.

Some say my first word was "data". I have been a data modeler for over 30 years and have taught variations of my **Data Modeling Master Class** since 1992—currently up to the 10th Edition! I have written nine books on data modeling, including *The Rosedata Stone* and *Data Modeling Made Simple*. I review data models using my Data Model Scorecard® technique. I am the founder of the Design Challenges group, creator of the Data Modeling Institute's Data Modeling Certification exam, Conference Chair of the Data Modeling Zone conferences, director of Technics Publications, lecturer at Columbia University, and recipient of the Data Administration Management Association (DAMA) International Professional Achievement Award.

Thinking of my daughter's brownie analogy, I have perfected the store-bought brownie recipe. That is, I know how to model. However, I am not an expert in every database solution.

That is why each book in this series combines my proven data modeling practices with database solution experts. So, for this book, Beda Hammerschmidt, Pascal Desmarets, and I are making the brownie together. I work on the store-bought brownie piece, and Beda and Pascal work on adding the chocolate chips and other delicious ingredients. Beda and Pascal are thought leaders when it comes to JSON in databases.

Beda Hammerschmidt studied computer science and later earned a PhD in indexing in XML databases. He joined Oracle as a software developer in 2006. He initiated the support for JSON in Oracle and is co-author of the SQL/JSON standard. Beda currently manages the groups supporting semi-structured data in Oracle (JSON, XML, Full Text, etc.).

Pascal Desmarets is the founder and CEO of Hackolade (https://hackolade.com), a data modeling tool for NoSQL databases, storage formats, REST APIs, and JSON in RDBMS. Hackolade pioneered Polyglot Data Modeling, which is data modeling for polyglot data persistence and data exchanges. With Hackolade's Metadata-as-Code strategy, data models are co-located with application code in Git repositories as they evolve and are published to business-facing data catalogs to ensure a shared understanding of the meaning and context of your data. We used Hackolade Studio software to create most of the entity-relationship diagrams in this book.

We hope our tag team approach shows you how to model any Oracle solution. Particularly for those with experience in data modeling of relational databases, the book provides a bridge from the traditional methods to the very different way we model to leverage the benefits of JSON-relational duality views with Oracle Database 23ai.

Oracle, the company, the products

Oracle is primarily known for developing and marketing database software and technology, but it has also expanded its product portfolio to include a wide range of enterprise software solutions.

Oracle's flagship product is the Oracle Database, a relational database management system (RDBMS) that is widely used by organizations around the world to store, manage, and retrieve data. The Oracle Database is known for its robustness, scalability, and security features, and it supports a variety of operating systems. The latest release of Oracle Database is called '23ai' and this release is the base for this book. Previous releases, like 19c, do have rich support for JSON but do not support JSON-relational duality.

In addition to the Oracle Database, the company offers various other software products and services, including:

- **Oracle Cloud Infrastructure (OCI):** a comprehensive suite of cloud services, including infrastructure as a service (IaaS), platform as a service (PaaS), and software as a service (SaaS);

- **Oracle Java:** the programming language and the tools, frameworks, and platforms for Java development;

- **Oracle Fusion Middleware:** a platform for the integration of different enterprise applications and systems;

- **Oracle Enterprise Resource Planning:** offers ERP software that helps organizations manage their core business processes, such as financial management, supply chain management, and human capital management.

The Autonomous Database combines advanced machine learning and automation capabilities to deliver a self-driving, self-securing, and self-repairing database management system. This eliminates the need for manual database administration tasks and significantly reduces human error by automating many traditionally time-consuming and complex processes. For JSON workloads, there is a variant called the Autonomous JSON Database.

JSON support in the Oracle Database

Oracle introduced support for JSON data and JSON-related functions starting from Oracle Database 12c, more precisely release 12.1.0.2. With this support, developers could store, index, query, manipulate, and generate JSON documents within the database, treating JSON data as a native data type alongside traditional relational data – for example, by storing JSON data in the column of a table.

A rich set of SQL functions and operators allows us to work with JSON data, including JSON parsing, indexing, querying, and manipulation. Oracle has contributed most SQL/JSON functions to the ISO SQL Standard. With version 23ai, Oracle introduced more JSON capabilities like JSON Schema (to validate JSON data and to describe database objects) and also a major innovation called "JSON-relational duality," which allows us to treat data both as tables as well as JSON documents. The data modeling of JSON-relational duality is the main subject of this book. But let's first review specific aspects of JSON documents.

The JSON document model

The document model refers to the way data is organized and stored within a database. This document model is vastly different than the relational model, so it deserves a formal explanation.

JSON (JavaScript Object Notation) is a lightweight, human-readable format used to interchange and store data. JSON provides a simple and flexible way to represent structured data as key-value pairs, arrays, and nested structures. JSON is easy for humans to read and write, and it is widely supported by programming languages and frameworks.

JSON is self-describing: each document contains both the data itself and information about its structure and content. In a JSON object, data is represented as key-value pairs, where the key is a string representing the data field's name, and the value can be a string, number, Boolean, array, or another JSON object. As JSON arrays and JSON objects can be nested (recursively), it is possible to create arbitrary hierarchies, making it possible to map any application object (e.g., Java object) to and from JSON.

Each value's type is explicitly defined, allowing applications to interpret the data accurately without relying on external schemas or metadata.

This inherent structure and type information make JSON easy for both humans and machines to understand and process without the need for additional explanations or documentation. That is, only if each key can be unambiguously defined and accurately understood by all stakeholders, which is where data modeling comes into play.

JSON's popularity for data storage has grown due to its compatibility with modern application development practices and the need to handle diverse data structures efficiently.

A JSON document is the basic unit of data (like a row in a relational database) and can include nesting to represent complex data structures.

Developers embrace the document model because it is flexible and can dynamically evolve.

As we will see in the book, this power comes with great responsibility, as it can easily become messy if not managed carefully, ideally with a data modeling tool like Hackolade.

There are two key features that are 'built into' JSON and which are hard or inefficient to model with tabular rows of traditional Relational Database Management Systems (RDBMS): hierarchical structures and polymorphism. Let's review both.

Hierarchical structure in documents

Documents organize values in a hierarchical (tree-like) structure. This is in contrast to the relational model, which consists of tables that are not in a fixed relationship, especially not one where a table exists 'under' or 'over' another table. Instead, tables exist independently and can be accessed (queried, updated) independently. Usually, any reasonably complex object will require multiple tables to hold all information and hence, joins are required to reassemble the object from the data stored in rows and columns. The fact that tables are independent yields a lot of flexibility as new and arbitrary objects can be assembled depending on the selected column values and how they're joined together. This makes the relational model ideal for applications with multiple use cases. For example, if different reports have to be generated from the same underlying tables. For cases where the objects are usually assembled the same way, the joins impose a performance penalty as they require finding the correct rows in different tables.

JSON documents with embedded (or nested) subobjects can be viewed as already joined. Therefore, no join operation is needed when fetching the document from a database. But this simplification comes with some consequences:

- The hierarchy is fixed. Unlike the relational model, which can assemble differently shaped outputs, a JSON document stores the data in one hierarchy.

- When fetching a document from the database, it contains all fields. Unlike a relational model, where you can select only those column values that are needed, a JSON document contains all information, and processing is needed if some value needs to be hidden.

- All access to an embedded (nested) subobject has to go through the root of the document, whereas, in the relational model, one can directly access the table of interest and leave out others.

The above points are inherent to the hierarchical data model and apply to all flavors, whether JSON or XML (or IMS).

If documents are trees, the relational model can be viewed as a graph or network. Data is organized in rows and columns of different tables that can be accessed independently and directly. The same values in columns are used to join tables to assemble the output data.

A major benefit of the relational model is that it does not require the developer to define a fixed hierarchy. Operations work with the relevant columns from only those tables that are needed for a specific use case.

The disadvantage of the relational model is that a single application object typically maps to multiple tables (instead of one object). Consequently, simple operations in the application code (like storing an order) require multiple database operations as data is decomposed on an insert and reassembled when reading it back. This also impacts the performance of complex application objects mapped to many rows in multiple tables.

Aside from the traditional "scalar" data types (string, numeric, Boolean, null), it is possible to use what is known as "complex" data types: objects and arrays. In JSON, an object is a collection of key-value pairs enclosed in curly braces {}. See Figure 1.

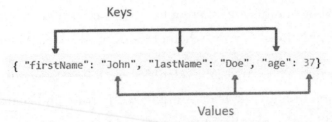

Figure 1: JSON object.

The keys are always strings, and the values can be any valid JSON data type, including another object, an array, a string, a number, a Boolean, or null.

```
{
  "name": "John Smith",
  "age": 35,
  "address": {
    "street": "123 Main St",
    "city": "Anytown",
    "state": "CA",
    "zip": "12345"
  }
}
```

Unlike in XML, JSON scalar value's data type is known without a schema: strings are enclosed in double quotes (like "CA" or "12345" in the above examples), numeric values are not quoted (for example, 35), and there are three unquoted non-numeric values: true, false, and null.

Note: JSON has no data types for common programming language types like dates, timestamps, or different numeric types. Binary JSON formats like Oracle's OSON or MongoDB's BSON provide a richer type system so that the mapping to JSON does not lose type information.

A JSON array is an ordered list of values enclosed in square brackets []. The values can be any valid JSON data type, including another array, an object, a string, a number, a Boolean, or null. A comma separates each value in the array. For example:

```
["apple", "banana", "orange", "grape"]
```

Figure 2 shows you can combine objects and arrays at will.

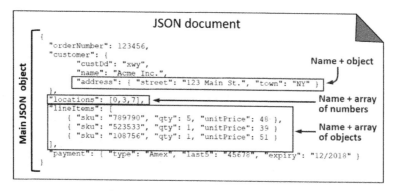

Figure 2: Combining objects at will.

For example, you may use an array of objects to embed another table into a document. The array models the one-to-many relationship between two tables.

Many-to-many relationships are a challenge in the hierarchical data model of JSON. You can model a many-to-many relationship as two one-to-many relationships in the corresponding documents (leading to data duplication, potential inconsistencies, and complex updates), or decide not to embed the actual data but use object identifiers instead (also leading to more complex updates and potential inconsistencies). We will learn later how JSON Duality solved this problem elegantly without data duplication and update challenges.

A JSON object consists of zero, one, or multiple key-value pairs which are unordered. Generally, in a JSON key-value pair, the key is a static name. It is also possible to have variable names for the key:

```
{
    "followers": {
        "abc123": {
            "name": "John Doe",
            "sports": ["tennis"]
        },
        "xyz987": {
            "name": "Joe Blow",
            "sports": ["cycling", "football"]
        }
    }
}
```

Grouping data in JSON with hierarchical subobjects and arrays can provide several benefits:

- **Improved data organization**: nesting related data with subobjects and arrays makes it easier to understand, navigate, query, and manipulate data.

- **Flexibility**: a more flexible data model can evolve and adapt to changing requirements more easily.

- **Improved performance**: embedding subdocuments within a parent document can improve performance by reducing the number of joins required to retrieve the data.

- **Better data representation**: for example, a customer object can contain a nested address object. In this way, it is clear that the address is related to the customer, and it is also more readable and intuitive.

- **Data integrity**: by keeping related data together, for example, each order can contain an array of cart items. This way, it is clear that the orders and items are related, and it is also easy to update all related data when required, as well as perform cascading deletes.

- **Developer convenience**: by aggregating structures to match objects to be manipulated in object-oriented programming, developers are more efficient by avoiding what's known as "object impedance mismatch", a common issue when working with relational databases.

Let's use the simple example of an order to fully visualize the above benefits and why users embrace the document model as an intuitive alternative to the traditional relational database structure.

With the relational model respecting the rules of normalization, we split the different components of an order into different tables at storage time. When retrieving the data, joins allow us to reassemble the different pieces for processing, display, or reporting. This is counter-intuitive for the common human (i.e., someone not trained in Third Normal Form) and expensive in terms of performance, particularly at scale. See Figure 3.

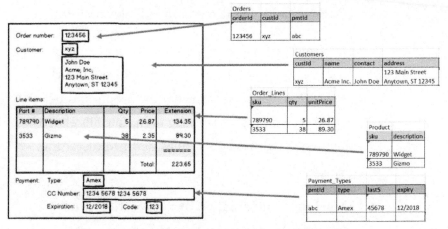

Figure 3: Relational representation of a business object.

With a JSON document, however, all the pieces of information that belong together are stored and retrieved together in a single document, an example appearing in Figure 4.

Nesting can provide the benefits described above, but it can also sometimes make data more complex and harder to work with if it's not properly organized and structured. And since there are no rules of normalization to serve as guardrails, data modeling is even more important than with relational databases.

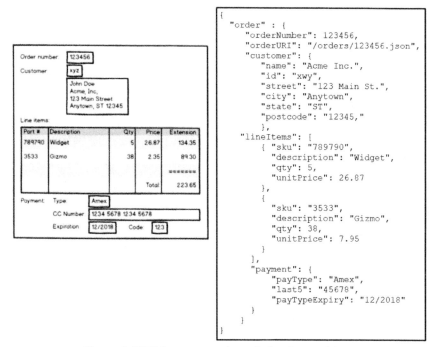

Figure 4: JSON representation of a business object.

Nesting subobjects and arrays to denormalize data to represent relationships can also increase the storage requirements. Still, with the minimal cost of storage these days, this drawback is often considered marginal. If data needs to be stored redundantly (for example, because the same value occurs in different documents or different parts of the same document), then it also increases storage requirements but even worse: it makes updates harder and opens the possibility of inconsistencies as the application has to make sure that all occurrences of the same data are modifies consistently.

Just like XSD defines elements and structures that can appear in XML documents, JSON Schema (https://json-schema.org/) defines how a JSON document should be structured, making it easy to ensure that it is formatted correctly. Hackolade Studio uses JSON Schema as an internal notation mechanism, so it dynamically generates JSON Schema for structures created with the tool without the user needing to be familiar with the JSON Schema syntax. Oracle database has a tool called *JSON Dataguide*, which can derive a JSON Schema from JSON documents stored in the database and outputs the information as a JSON Schema document. This schema can be used for validation or with a tool like Hackolade Studio to improve or redesign the data model.

To decide whether to use or avoid, developers should weigh the benefits and drawbacks of nesting data and make an informed decision. Later in this book, the section about the different schema design patterns provides many details to help make informed decisions.

Polymorphism

Polymorphism in JSON refers to the ability of a JSON object to take on multiple forms. There are various degrees of polymorphism in JSON documents to serve different use cases.

Fields with multiple data types

The simplest case of polymorphism in JSON is when a field can have different data types, for example:

```
{
  "raceResults": [
      {
        "Position": 1,
        "Driver": "Lewis Hamilton"
      },
      {
        "Position": 2,
        "Driver": "Max Verstappen"
      },
      {
        "Position": "DNF",
        "Driver": "Charles Leclerc"
      }
  ]
}
```

The "Position" field can have different data types depending on the race result: numeric for rank or string for non-rank status such as DNS (Did Not Start), DNF (Did Not Finish), or DSQ (Disqualified).

Multiple document types in the same collection

A more complex case of polymorphism is when different documents in the same collection have different shapes, similar to table inheritance in relational databases. Specifically, it refers to the ability of a JSON object to have different properties or fields, depending on the type of data it represents.

For example, consider a table for bank accounts. Several types of bank accounts are possible: checking, savings, and loan. There is a structure common to all types, and a structure specific to each type. For example, a document for a checking account might look like this:

```
{
  "accountNumber": "123456789",
  "balance": 1000,
  "accountType": "checking",
  "accountDetails": {
    "minimumBalance": 100,
    "overdraftLimit": 500
  }
}
```

Another document for a savings account might look like this:

```
{
  "accountNumber": "987654321",
  "balance": 5000,
  "accountType": "savings",
  "accountDetails": {
    "interestRate": 0.05,
    "interestEarned": 115.26
  }
}
```

And for a loan account, a document might look like this:

```
{
  "accountNumber": "567890123",
  "balance": -5916.06,
  "accountType": "loan",
```

```
"accountDetails": {
  "loanAmount": 10000,
  "term": 36,
  "interestRate": 1.5,
  "monthlyPmt": 291.71
}
}
```

This flexible and dynamic structure is very convenient and eliminates the need for separate tables or wide tables that quickly become unmanageable at scale.

However, this flexibility can also create challenges when querying or manipulating the data, as it requires applications to account for variations in data types and structure. Without going into details at this stage, Figure 5 shows a single schema for these documents.

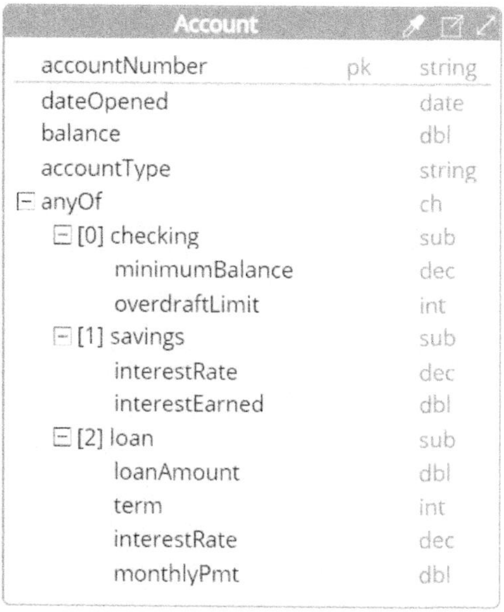

Account		
accountNumber	pk	string
dateOpened		date
balance		dbl
accountType		string
⊟ anyOf		ch
⊟ [0] checking		sub
minimumBalance		dec
overdraftLimit		int
⊟ [1] savings		sub
interestRate		dec
interestEarned		dbl
⊟ [2] loan		sub
loanAmount		dbl
term		int
interestRate		dec
monthlyPmt		dbl

Figure 5: Single schema.

For those familiar with traditional data modeling, the above would be represented with subtypes and could result in table inheritance, as shown in Figure 6.

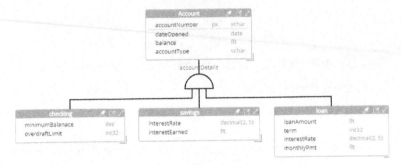

Figure 6: Subtyping.

Schema evolution and versioning

Another common case of polymorphism is when documents have different shapes within the same collection, due to the progressive evolution of the document schema over time. This could be done implicitly, or with an explicit version number as part of the root-level fields of the document.

Developers love the fact that schema evolution is easy with the document model. You can add or remove fields, change data types, modify indexing options, etc., to accommodate new or changing requirements without the headaches that such changes would imply with relational databases.

The schema versioning pattern is described in detail later in this book. For now, it is enough to know that this pattern leverages the polymorphic capabilities of the document model.

We should manage schema evolution and versioning carefully to avoid technical debt and to consider that data may be read by different applications and SQL or BI tools that cannot handle this polymorphism. Schema migration is a best practice in successful projects and organizations leveraging NoSQL and, therefore, should be part of the schema evolution strategy to mitigate the drawbacks.

JSON-relational duality

A physics affine reader may think about light where duality means that light is both a wave and a particle. This analogy holds for data: with JSON-relational duality, data is both a document and table at the same time (without data duplication).

Before we explain how JSON-relational duality works, let's reiterate the characteristics of JSON documents and tables:

JSON:

+ Easy to work with (human readable, self-describing).

+ Schema is flexible and easy to add new data and evolve.

+ Document (usually) includes all data required for a use

case, reducing round trips from the application to the databases.

+ Maps easily to application objects.

- Finding a single hierarchy for all use cases is challenging or not possible, leading to redundant data storage, inconsistencies, and complex update logic.

- Queries have to follow the document hierarchy to access embedded or nested data. Direct access is only possible if data gets replicated.

Relational tables:

+ Data is stored once, avoiding redundancies. Updates only need to change on the value, therefore avoiding inconsistencies.

+ The names of data values are static table properties (column names) and are not repeated for every row.

+ Queries select only the relevant parts of a row, reducing the amount of data transferred to the applications.

+ The relational model is very *query flexible*: queries can perform arbitrary joins across different tables to assemble new output information.

- The relational model is not very *storage flexible*: it is harder to evolve the schema if new values need to be stored, if values can have different data types, or if the cardinality of a relationship changes.

- Requires upfront schema normalization and SQL knowledge.

With Oracle database release 23ai, Oracle introduces a new paradigm to unite both approaches, hence combining the benefits of normalized tables with the JSON document model.

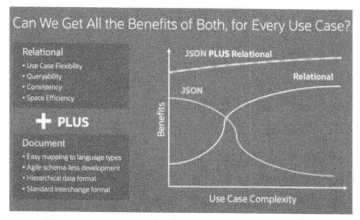

Figure 7: Benefits of both relational and document.

The convergence of the traditional relational/normalized approach with the more recent JSON document approach creates a combination worth more than the sum of the parts.

The core idea of JSON-relational duality is actually very simple: treat JSON documents not as persistent objects but as 'transient': views that assemble the value in use case-specific hierarchies. The key here is that you can have infinitely many views, they can share common values, and they're updateable!

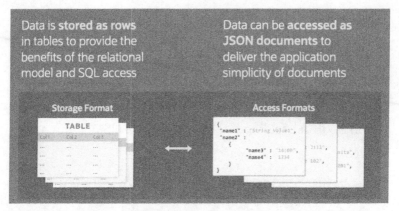

Figure 8: How it works.

Although this approach requires the user to normalize data and create tables, this step is actually quite natural as the user typically understands the *entities* of the application. For example, a shop application consists of orders, customers, products, and so on. The entities naturally map to tables, and known attributes (like customer name and order date) map to columns in this table. Where the relational model falls a bit short is that perfect knowledge is required when creating tables, as adding new columns are painful. JSON Duality supports a so-called flex column, which allows additional key-value pairs in a JSON document to map to a JSON column in the corresponding table. For example, an update on a customer's document could add the new field 'middleName' which was never declared when first creating the table.

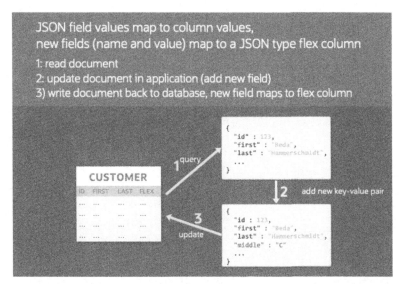

Figure 9: About flex columns.

Therefore, JSON duality supports schema flexibility and application evolution similarly to a pure JSON document database.

But where JSON-relational duality really rocks is the ability to share the same value in different JSON documents! Because the actual data (the values) reside in tables, and we can create multiple JSON duality views, it is possible to refer to the same value from different documents. For example, an 'order' document contains a 'customer' sub-object. In a pure document database that stores JSON persistently, one would have to duplicate the customer data or just store a customer's id (preventing the customer's information from being visible and requiring another roundtrip to the database to fetch the customer with the given id). With JSON-relational duality, we can embed a customer's information in as many duality views as we want. The actual data is only stored once, making updates simple (only one place needs to be updated) and making inconsistencies impossible.

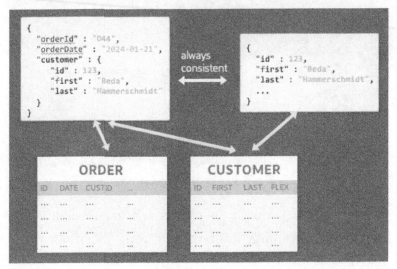

Figure 10: How data stays consistent.

Another built-in benefit of Oracle's JSON-relational duality is the optimistic concurrency control for applications where the locking of documents (or rows) is not a good idea: either because of stateless mid-tiers like REST (a lock may never be released) or applications with large number of concurrent users.

We implement optimistic locking in JSON duality by calculating a 'checksum' of the values and embedding it into the object returned by a JSON duality view. An application can modify an object, and when it sends it back to the database, the checksum (called 'etag') of the document is compared against the checksum of the values in the database. If they do not match, then someone else has performed a conflicting change and the update is aborted (preventing overwriting someone else's changes).

Because the checksum (etag) is value-based, it also detects 'sideband updates', which are updates through other duality views or even direct table updates through SQL. You can work with the same data using JSON documents as well as plain old SQL operations!

In Figure 11, two concurrent updates conflict: the application changes the name but leaves the state unchanged. A SQL sideband update modifies the state column of the row that maps to the object.

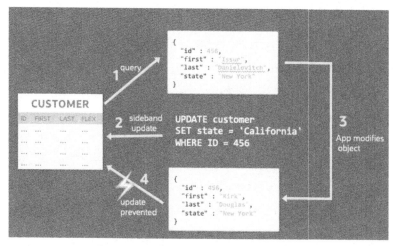

Figure 11: The state remains unchanged.

So JSON-relational duality offers the benefits of both JSON documents and the relational model while mitigating their limitations.

A JSON document represents an application object directly, capturing its hierarchical relationships and eliminating the need for external references or schemas.

On the other hand, the relational model decomposes application objects into normalized tables, enabling efficient and correct data combinations through joins. Each JSON-relational duality view exposes relational data as JSON documents, dynamically generating them when needed and in the shape (and hierarchy) that the developer prefers for this use case. Columns that are not needed or should not be shown (like a salary) can be omitted from one view but be part of another.

This approach provides both relational and hierarchical organization for the data, allowing applications to access and manipulate it in either JSON or relational form simultaneously. Duality views act as a unified persistence format for application objects, applicable to all clients and eliminating the need for separate mappers. The views present the same data in both table and document aspects, empowering server-side manipulation of relational data and simplifying JSON handling on the client side.

While we concentrate on the impact of data modeling in this book, you may read more about duality views in this document: : https://tinyurl.com/wsma5a4u.

A typical characteristic of a NoSQL document database is that the schema is not enforced. This feature has pros and cons. The flexibility and easy evolution of the JSON document model shift the responsibility to enforce constraints from the database to the application. Hence, the developer ensures the data remains consistent and conforms to application requirements. Unless there is much rigor and coordination on all fronts, this situation can quickly lead to data corruption, inaccurate query results, slow performance, and hard-to-debug application errors.

With Oracle Duality Views, it is possible to maintain data integrity thanks to the relational model while providing developers with JSON objects to manipulate easily in application code.

SQL/JSON

SQL/JSON is a set of SQL language extensions introduced in the 2016 release of the ISO SQL standard (future releases of the standard will contain more JSON enhancements, such as a JSON data type, which Oracle included since release 21c). SQL/JSON is an extension to the SQL language that provides native support for querying, manipulating, and generating JSON data within the context of a relational database.

With SQL/JSON, users can combine the power of SQL, which is primarily designed for working with structured tabular data, with the flexibility and versatility of JSON. It enables developers to seamlessly integrate JSON data into their SQL queries, treating JSON objects and arrays as first-class data types.

The SQL/JSON standard defines a range of SQL functions and operators specifically tailored for handling JSON data. These functions and operators allow operations such as JSON parsing, navigation, querying, filtering, and aggregation. Users can extract specific data elements from JSON documents, filter results based on JSON properties or values, and perform complex transformations and manipulations on JSON data.

SQL/JSON also introduces the concept of JSON path expressions, which you can use to navigate and reference specific elements within a JSON document. JSON path expressions resemble XPath expressions and allow granular querying and manipulation of JSON data.

If JSON data is stored in a relational database with SQL/JSON support (like Oracle), then it's also possible to join JSON data with other data like relational or XML or to generate JSON data from relational sources. Another benefit of storing JSON in a relational database is that other capabilities like transactions, user grants, security features, or the optimizer also apply for JSON.

GraphQL

GraphQL is a relatively new standard for an API query language (https://spec.graphql.org/). Unlike SQL, GraphQL has not yet found broad use in databases, so it is great that Oracle supports GraphQL as one way to define a duality view. This book will use SQL/JSON to show examples of duality views as more people are familiar with SQL syntax. A reader with GraphQL experience can easily use the shorter GraphQL instead.

Data modeling and schema design

As you can imagine, data modeling and schema design for the document model differ greatly from the relational model. That's because JSON-like documents are denormalized documents with nested objects and arrays instead of normalized flat tables.

Data modeling is a crucial step in the development process, as it allows developers to work closely with subject matter experts to define the structure of the data before any coding begins. Just as a recipe guides the baking of brownies, a data model serves as a blueprint for the structure and organization of data. By involving subject matter experts in the modeling process, developers can ensure that the data model accurately reflects the needs and requirements of the project. With such collaboration, developers are more likely to avoid potential mistakes and inconsistencies arising from working with poorly defined data. By following a recipe before starting to bake, developers can be more efficient and successful in creating a product that meets the needs of the end-user.

Audience

We wrote this book for two audiences:

- Data architects and modelers who need to expand their modeling skills to include Oracle Duality Views. That is, those of us who know how to make a store-bought brownie but are looking for those secret additions like chocolate chips.

- Database administrators and developers who know Oracle but need to expand their modeling skills. That is, those of us who know the value of chocolate chips and other ingredients, but need to learn how to combine these ingredients with those store-bought brownie mixes.

This book contains a foundational introduction followed by three approach-driven chapters. Think of the introduction as making that store-built brownie and the subsequent chapters as adding chocolate chips and other yummy ingredients. More on these four sections:

- **Introduction: About Data Models**. This overview covers the three modeling characteristics of precise, minimal, and visual; the three model components of entities, relationships, and attributes; the three model levels of conceptual (align), logical (refine), and physical (design); and the three modeling perspectives of relational, dimensional, and query. By the end of this introduction, you will know data modeling concepts and how to approach any data modeling assignment. This introduction will be useful to database administrators and developers who need a foundation in data modeling, as well as data architects and data modelers who need a modeling refresher.

- **Chapter 1: Align**. This chapter will explain the data modeling align phase. We explain the purpose of aligning our business vocabulary, introduce our animal shelter case study, and then walk through the align approach. This chapter will be useful for both audiences, architects/modelers and database administrators/developers.

- **Chapter 2: Refine**. This chapter will explain the data modeling refine phase. We explain the purpose of refine, refine the model for our animal shelter case study, and then walk through the refine approach. This chapter will be useful for both audiences, architects/modelers and database administrators/developers.

- **Chapter 3: Design**. This chapter will explain the data modeling design phase. We explain the purpose of design, design the model for our animal shelter case study, and then walk through the design approach. This chapter will be useful for both audiences, architects/modelers and database administrators/developers.

We end each chapter with three tips and three takeaways. We aim to write as concisely yet comprehensively as possible to make the most of your time.

Most data models throughout the book were created using Hackolade Studio (https://hackolade.com) and are accessible for reference at https://github.com/hackolade/books along with additional sample data models to play with.

Let's begin!

Beda, Pascal, and Steve

About Data Models

T his chapter is all about making that store-built brownie. We present the data modeling principles and concepts within a single chapter. In addition to explaining the data model, this chapter covers the three modeling characteristics of precise, minimal, and visual; the three model components of entities, relationships, and attributes; the three model levels of conceptual (align), logical (refine), and physical (design); and the three modeling perspectives of relational, dimensional, and query. By the end of this chapter, you will know how to approach any data modeling assignment.

Data model explanation

A model is a precise representation of a landscape. Precise means there is only one way to read a model—it is not ambiguous nor up to interpretation. You and I read the same model the exact same way, making the model an extremely valuable communication tool.

We need to 'speak' a language before we can discuss content. That is, once we know how to read the symbols on a model (syntax), we can discuss what the symbols represent (semantics).

Once we understand the syntax, we can discuss the semantics.

For example, a map like the one in Figure 12 helps a visitor navigate a city. Once we know what the symbols mean on a map, such as lines representing streets, we can read the map and use it as a valuable navigation tool for understanding a geographical landscape.

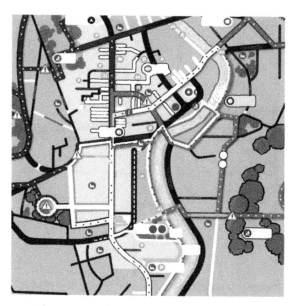

Figure 12: Map of a geographic landscape.

A blueprint like the one in Figure 13 helps an architect communicate building plans. The blueprint, too, contains only representations, such as rectangles for rooms and lines for pipes. Once we know what the rectangles and lines mean on a blueprint, we know what the structure will look like and can understand the architectural landscape.

The data model like the one in Figure 14 helps business professionals and technologists discuss requirements and terminology. The data model, too, contains only representations, such as rectangles for terms and lines for business rules. Once we know what the rectangles and lines mean on a data model, we can debate and eventually agree on the business requirements and terminology captured in the informational landscape.

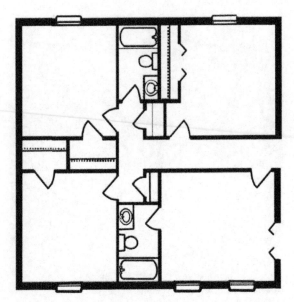

Figure 13: Map of an architectural landscape.

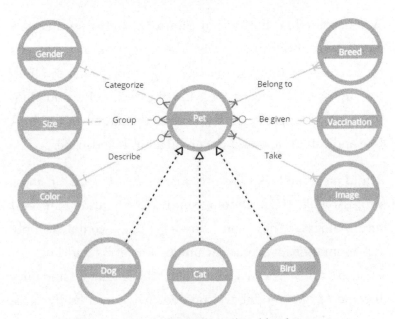

Figure 14: Map of an informational landscape.

A data model is a precise representation of an information landscape. We build data models to confirm and document our understanding of other perspectives.

In addition to precision, two other important characteristics of the model are minimal and visual. Let's discuss all three characteristics.

Three model characteristics

Models are valuable because they are precise—there is only one way to interpret the symbols on the model. We must transform the ambiguity in our verbal and sometimes written communication into a precise language. Precision does not mean complex—we need to keep our language simple and show the minimal amount needed for successful communication. In addition, following the maxim "a picture is worth a thousand words," we need visuals to communicate this precise and simple language for the initiative.

Precise, minimal, and visual are three essential characteristics of the model.

Precise

Bob: How's your course going?

Mary: Going well. But my students are complaining about too much homework. They tell me they have many other classes.

Bob: The attendees in my advanced session say the same thing.

Mary: I wouldn't expect that from graduates. Anyway, how many other offerings are you teaching this semester?

Bob: I'm teaching five offerings this term and one is an evening not-for-credit class.

We can let this conversation continue for a few pages, but do you see the ambiguity caused by this simple dialog?

- What is the difference between **Course**, **Class**, **Offering**, and **Session**?
- Are **Semester** and **Term** the same?
- Are **Student** and **Attendee** the same?

Precision means "exactly or sharply defined or stated." Precision means there is only one interpretation for a term, including the term's name, definition, and connections to other terms. Most issues organizations face related to growth, credibility, and saving lives, stem from a lack of precision.

On a recent project, Steve needed to explain data modeling to a group of senior human resource executives. These very high-level managers lead departments responsible for implementing a very expensive global employee expense system. Steve felt the last thing these busy human resource executives needed was a lecture on data modeling. So instead, he asked each of these managers sitting around this large boardroom table to write down their definition of an employee. After a few minutes, most of the writing stopped and he asked them to share their definitions of an employee.

As expected, no two definitions were the same. For example, one manager included contingency workers in his definition, while another included summer interns. Instead of spending the remaining meeting time attempting to come to a consensus on the meaning of an employee, we discussed the reasons we create data models, including the value of precision. Steve explained that after we complete the difficult journey of achieving the agreed-upon employee definition and document it in the form of a data model, no one will ever have to go through the same painful process again. Instead, they can use and build upon the existing model, adding even more value for the organization.

Making terms precise is hard work. We need to transform the ambiguity in our verbal and sometimes written communication into a form where five people can read about the term and each gets a single clear picture of the term, not five different interpretations. For example, a group of business users initially define **Product** as:

Something we produce intending to sell for profit.

Is this definition precise? If you and I read this definition, are we each clear on what *something* means? Is *something* tangible like a hammer or instead some type of service? If it is a hammer and we donate this hammer to a not-for-profit organization, is it still a hammer? After all, we didn't make a *profit* on it. The word *intending* may cover us, but still, shouldn't this word be explained in more detail? And who is *we*? Is it our entire organization or maybe just a subset? What does *profit* really mean anyway? Can two people read the word *profit* and see it very differently?

You see the problem. We need to think like detectives to find gaps and ambiguous statements in the text and make terms precise. After some debate, we update our **Product** definition to:

A product, also known as a finished product, is something that is in a state to be sold to a consumer. It has completed the manufacturing process, contains a wrapper, and is labeled for resale. A product is different than a raw material and a semi-finished good. A raw material, such as sugar or milk, and a semi-finished good, such as melted chocolate, is never sold to a consumer. If, in the future, sugar or milk is sold directly to consumers, than sugar and milk become products.

Examples:
Widgets Dark Chocolate 42 oz
Lemonizer 10 oz
Blueberry pickle juice 24 oz

Ask at least five people to see if they are all clear on this particular initiative's definition of a product. The best way to test precision is to try to break the definition. Think of lots of examples and see if everyone makes the same decision as to whether the examples are products or not.

In 1967, G.H. Mealy wrote a white paper where he said:

> We do not, it seems, have a very clear and commonly agreed upon set of notions about data—either what they are, how they should be fed and cared for, or their relation to the design of programming languages and operating systems.[1]

---

[1] G. H. Mealy, "Another Look at Data," AFIPS, pp. 525-534, 1967 Proceedings of the Fall Joint Computer Conference, 1967. http://tw.rpi.edu/media/2013/11/11/134fa/GHMealy-1967-FJCC-p525.pdf.

Although Mr. Mealy made this claim over 50 years ago, if we replace *programming languages and operating systems* with the word *databases*, we can make a similar claim today.

Aiming for precision can help us better understand our business terms and business requirements.

Minimal

The world around us is full of obstacles that can overwhelm our senses, making it very challenging to focus only on the relevant information needed to make intelligent decisions. Therefore, the model contains a minimal set of symbols and text, simplifying a subset of the real world by only including representations of what we need to understand. Much is filtered out on a model, creating an incomplete but extremely useful reflection of reality. For example, we might need to communicate descriptive information about **Customer**, such as their name, birth date, and email address. But we will not include information on the process of adding or deleting a customer.

Visuals

Visuals mean that we need a picture instead of lots of text. Our brains process images 60,000 times faster than text, and

90 percent of the information transmitted to the brain is visual.[2]

We might read an entire document but not reach that moment of clarity until we see a figure or picture summarizing everything. Imagine reading directions to navigate from one city to another versus the ease of reading a map that shows visually how the roads connect.

Three model components

The three components of a data model are entities, relationships, and attributes (including keys).

Entities

An entity is a collection of information about something important to the business. It is a noun considered basic and critical to your audience for a particular initiative. Basic means this entity is mentioned frequently in conversations while discussing the initiative. Critical means the initiative would be very different or non-existent without this entity.

---

[2] https://www.t-sciences.com/news/humans-process-visual-data-better.

The majority of entities are easy to identify and include nouns that are common across industries, such as **Customer**, **Employee**, and **Product**. Entities can have different names and meanings within departments, organizations, or industries based on audience and initiative (scope). An airline may call a **Customer** a *Passenger*, a hospital may call a **Customer** a *Patient*, an insurance company may call a **Customer** a *Policyholder*, yet they are all recipients of goods or services.

Each entity fits into one of six categories: who, what, when, where, why, or how. That is, each entity is either a who, what, when, where, why, or how. Table 1 contains a definition of each of these categories, along with examples.

We traditionally show entities as rectangles on a data model, such as these two for our animal shelter:

Pet	Breed

Figure 15: Traditional entities.

Entity instances are the occurrences, examples, or representatives of that entity. The entity **Pet** may have multiple instances, such as Spot, Daisy, and Misty. The entity **Breed** may have multiple instances, such as German Shephard, Greyhound, and Beagle.

Category	Definition	Examples
Who	Person or organization of interest to the initiative.	Employee, Patient, Player, Suspect, Customer, Vendor, Student, Passenger, Competitor, Author
What	Product or service of interest to the initiative. What the organization makes or provides that keeps it in business.	Product, Service, Raw Material, Finished Good, Course, Song, Photograph, Tax Preparation, Policy, Breed
When	Calendar or time interval of interest to the initiative.	Schedule, Semester, Fiscal Period, Duration
Where	Location of interest to the initiative. Location can refer to actual places as well as electronic places.	Employee Home Address, Distribution Point, Customer Website
Why	Event or transaction of interest to the initiative.	Order, Return, Complaint, Withdrawal, Payment, Trade, Claim
How	Documentation of the event of interest to the initiative. Records events such as a Purchase Order (a "How") recording an Order event (a "Why"). A document provides evidence that an event took place.	Invoice, Contract, Agreement, Purchase Order, Speeding Ticket, Packing Slip, Trade Confirmation

Table 1: Entity categories plus examples.

Entities and entity instances take on more precise names when discussing specific technologies. For example, entities are tables and instances are rows in a RDBMS like Oracle.

Entities are collections and instances are documents in Oracle duality views.

Relationships

A relationship represents a business connection between two entities, and appears on the model traditionally as a line connecting two rectangles. For example, here is a relationship between **Pet** and **Breed**:

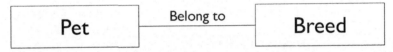

Figure 16: Relationship and label.

The phrase **Belong to** is called a *label*. A label adds meaning to the relationship. Instead of just saying that a **Pet** may relate to a **Breed**, we can say that a **Pet** may belong to a **Breed**. **Belong to** is more meaningful than **Relate**.

So far, we know that a relationship represents a business connection between two entities. It would be nice to know more about the relationship, such as whether a **Pet** may belong to more than one **Breed** or whether a **Breed** can categorize more than one **Pet**. Enter cardinality.

Cardinality means the additional symbols on the relationship line that communicate how many instances from one entity participate in the relationship with instances of the other entity.

There are several modeling notations, and each notation has its own set of symbols. Throughout this book, we use a notation called *Information Engineering (IE)*. The IE notation has been a very popular notation since the early 1980s. If you use a notation other than IE within your organization, you must translate the following symbols into the corresponding symbols in your modeling notation.

We can choose any combination of zero, one, or many for cardinality. *Many* (some people use "more") means one or more. Yes, many includes one. Specifying one or many allows us to capture *how many* of a particular entity instance participate in a given relationship. Specifying zero or one allows us to capture whether an entity instance is or is not required in a relationship.

Recall this relationship between **Pet** and **Breed**:

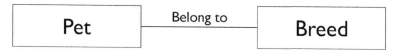

Figure 17: Relationship and label.

Let's now add cardinality.

We first ask the *Participation* questions to learn more. Participation questions tell us whether the relationship is 'one' or 'many'. So, for example:

- Can a **Pet** belong to more than one **Breed**?
- Can a **Breed** categorize more than one **Pet**?

A simple spreadsheet can keep track of these questions and their answers:

Question	Yes	No
Can a Pet belong to more than one Breed?		
Can a Breed categorize more than one Pet?		

We asked the animal shelter experts and received these answers:

Question	Yes	No
Can a Pet belong to more than one Breed?	✓	
Can a Breed categorize more than one Pet?	✓	

We learn that a **Pet** may belong to more than one **Breed**. For example, Daisy is part Beagle and part Terrier. We also learned that a **Breed** may categorize more than one **Pet**. Both Sparky and Spot are Greyhounds.

'Many' (meaning one or more) on a data model in the IE notation is a symbol that looks like a crow's foot (and is called a *crow's foot* by data folks). See Figure 18.

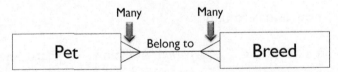

Figure 18: Displaying the answers to the Participation questions.

Now we know more about the relationship:

- Each **Pet** may belong to many **Breeds**.
- Each **Breed** may categorize many **Pets**.

We also always use the word 'each' when reading a relationship and start with the entity that makes the most sense to the reader, usually the one with the clearest relationship label.

This relationship is not yet precise, though. So, in addition to asking these two Participation questions, we also need to ask the *Existence* questions. Existence tells us for each relationship whether one entity can exist without the other term. For example:

- Can a **Pet** exist without a **Breed**?
- Can a **Breed** exist without a **Pet**?

We asked the animal shelter experts and received these answers:

Question	Yes	No
Can a Pet exist without a Breed?		✓
Can a Breed exist without a Pet?	✓	

So we learn that a **Pet** cannot exist without a **Breed**, and that a **Breed** can exist without a **Pet**. This means, for example, that we may not have any Chihuahuas in our animal shelter. Yet we need to capture a **Breed** (and in this case, one or more **Breeds**), for every **Pet**. As soon as we know about Daisy, we need to identify at least one of her breeds, such as Beagle or Terrier.

Figure 19 displays the answers to these two questions.

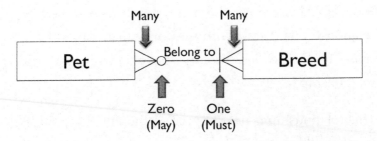

Figure 19: Displaying the answers to the Existence questions.

After adding existence, we have a precise relationship:

- Each **Pet** must belong to many **Breeds**.
- Each **Breed** may categorize many **Pets**.

The Existence questions are also known as the May/Must questions. The Existence questions tell us when reading the relationship, whether we say "may" or "must." A zero means "may", indicating optionality—the entity can exist without the other entity. A **Breed** *may* exist without a **Pet**, for example. A one means "must", indicating required—the entity cannot exist without the other entity. A **Pet** *must* belong to at least one **Breed**, for example.

There are two more questions to ask if we are working on the more detailed logical data model (which we will discuss shortly). These are the *Identification* questions.

Identification tells us for each relationship whether one entity can be identified without the other term. For example:

- Can a **Pet** be identified without a **Breed**?
- Can a **Breed** be identified without a **Pet**?

We asked the animal shelter experts and received these answers:

Question	Yes	No
Can a Pet be identified without a Breed?	✓	
Can a Breed be identified without a Pet?	✓	

So we learn that a **Pet** can be identified without knowing a **Breed**. We can identify the pet Sparky without knowing that Sparky is a German Shepherd. In addition, we can identify a **Breed** without knowing the **Pet**. This means, for example, that we can identify the Chihuahua breed without including any information from **Pet**.

A dotted line captures a non-identifying relationship. That is, when the answer to both questions is "yes". A solid line captures an identifying relationship. That is, when one of the answers is "no".

Non-identifying

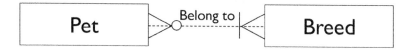

Identifying

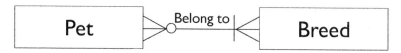

Figure 20: A non-identifying (top) and identifying (bottom) relationship.

So to summarize, the Participation questions reveal whether each entity has a one or many relationship to the other entity. The Existence questions reveal whether each entity has an optional ("may") or mandatory ("must") relationship to the other entity. The Identification questions reveal whether each entity requires the other entity to bring back a unique entity instance.

Use instances to make things clear in the beginning and eventually help you explain your models to colleagues. See Figure 21 for an example.

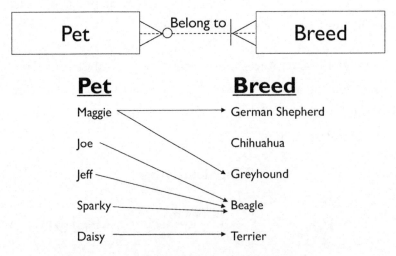

Figure 21: Use sample data to validate a relationship

You can see from this dataset that a **Pet** can belong to more than one **Breed**, such as Maggie being a German Shepherd/Greyhound mix. You can also see that every **Pet** must belong to at least one **Breed**. We could also have a **Breed** that is not categorizing any **Pets**, such as Chihuahua.

In addition, a **Breed** can categorize multiple **Pets**, such as Joe, Jeff, and Sparky are all Beagles.

Answering all six questions leads to a precise relationship. Precise means we all read the model the same exact way.

Let's say that we have slightly different answers to our six questions:

Question	Yes	No
Can a Pet belong to more than one Breed?		✓
Can a Breed categorize more than one Pet?	✓	
Can a Pet exist without a Breed?		✓
Can a Breed exist without a Pet?	✓	
Can a Pet be identified without a Breed?	✓	
Can a Breed be identified without a Pet?	✓	

These six answers lead to this model:

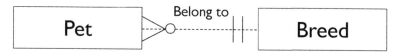

- Each **Pet** must belong to one **Breed**.
- Each **Breed** may categorize many **Pets**.

Figure 22: Different answers to the six questions lead to different cardinality.

On this model, we are only including pure-breed pets, as a **Pet** must be assigned one **Breed**. No mutts in our shelter!

Be very clear on labels. Labels are the verbs that connect our entities (nouns). To read any complete sentence, we need both nouns and verbs. Make sure the labels on the relationship lines are as descriptive as possible. Here are some examples of good labels:

- Contain
- Provide
- Own
- Initiate
- Characterize

Avoid the following words as labels, as they provide no additional information to the reader. You can use these words in combination with other words to make a meaningful label; just avoid using these words by themselves:

- Have
- Associate
- Participate
- Relate
- Are

For example, replace the relationship sentence:

"Each **Pet** must *relate to* one **Breed**."

With:

"Each **Pet** must *belong to* one **Breed**."

Relationships take on more precise names when discussing specific technologies. For example, relationships are constraints in a RDBMS such as Oracle. Relationships in Oracle duality views can be represented with references, but they are not enforceable constraints. It is often preferred to implement relationships through embedding. We will cover the pros and cons of both approaches shortly.

In addition to relationship lines, we can also have a subtyping relationship. The subtyping relationship groups common entities together. For example, the **Dog** and **Cat** entities might be grouped using subtyping under the more generic **Pet** term. In this example, **Pet** would be called the grouping entity or supertype, and **Dog** and **Cat** would be the terms that are grouped together, also known as the subtypes, as shown in Figure 23.

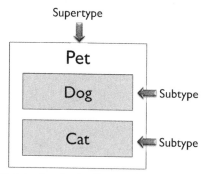

Figure 23: Subtyping is similar to the concept of inheritance.

We would read this model as:

- Each **Pet** may be either a **Dog** or a **Cat**.
- **Dog** is a **Pet**. **Cat** is a **Pet**.

The subtyping relationship means that all of the relationships (and attributes that we'll learn about shortly) that belong to the supertype from other terms also belong to each subtype. Therefore, the relationships to **Pet** also belong to **Dog** and **Cat**. So, for example, cats can be assigned breeds as well, so the relationship to **Breed** can exist at the **Pet** level instead of the **Dog** level, encompassing both cats and dogs. See Figure 24 for an example.

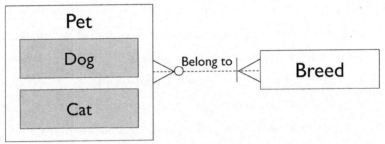

Figure 24: The relationship to Pet is inherited to Dog and Cat.

So the relationship:

- Each **Pet** must belong to many **Breeds**.
- Each **Breed** may categorize many **Pets**.

Also applies to **Dog** and **Cat**:

- Each **Dog** must belong to many **Breeds**.
- Each **Breed** may categorize many **Dogs**.
- Each **Cat** must belong to many **Breeds**.
- Each **Breed** may categorize many **Cats**.

Not only does subtyping reduce redundancy, but it also makes it easier to communicate similarities across what would appear to be distinct and separate terms.

Attributes and keys

An entity contains attributes. An *attribute* is an individual piece of information whose values identify, describe, or measure instances of an entity. The entity **Pet** might contain the attributes **Pet Number** that identifies the **Pet**, **Pet Name** that describes the **Pet**, and **Pet Age** that measures the **Pet.**

Attributes take on more precise names when discussing specific technologies. For example, attributes are columns in a RDBMS such as Oracle. Attributes are called fields in Oracle duality views.

A candidate key is one or more attributes that uniquely identify an entity instance. We assign a **ISBN** (International Standard Book Number) to every title. The **ISBN** uniquely identifies each title and is, therefore, the title's candidate key. **Tax ID** can be a candidate key for an organization in some countries, such as the United States. **Account Code** can be a candidate key for an account. A **VIN** (Vehicle Identification Number) identifies a vehicle.

A candidate key must be unique and mandatory. Unique means a candidate key value must not identify more than one entity instance (or one real-world thing). Mandatory means a candidate key cannot be empty (also known as *nullable*). Each entity instance must be identified by exactly one candidate key value.

The number of distinct values of a candidate key is always equal to the number of distinct entity instances. If the entity **Title** has **ISBN** as its candidate key, and if there are 500 title instances, there will also be 500 unique ISBNs.

Even though an entity may contain more than one candidate key, we can only select one candidate key to be the primary key for an entity. A primary key is the candidate key that has been chosen to be *the preferred* unique identifier for an entity. An alternate key is a candidate key that, although it has the properties of being unique and mandatory, was not chosen as the primary key. However, we can still use the alternate key to find specific entity instances.

The primary key appears above the line in the entity box, and the alternate key contains the 'AK' in parentheses. So, in Figure 25, **Pet Number** is the primary key and **Pet Name** is the alternate key. Having an alternate key on **Pet Name** means we cannot have two pets with the same name. Whether this can happen or not is a good discussion point. However, the model in its current state would not allow duplicate **Pet Names**.

Figure 25: An alternate key on Pet Name means we cannot have two pets with the same name.

A candidate key can be either simple, compound, or composite. If it is simple, it can be either business or surrogate. Table 2 contains examples of each key type.

	SIMPLE	COMPOUND	COMPOSITE	OVERLOADED
BUSINESS	ISBN	PROMOTION TYPE CODE + PROMOTION START DATE	(CUSTOMER FIRST NAME + CUSTOMER LAST NAME + BIRTHDAY)	STUDENT GRADE
SURROGATE	BOOK ID			

Table 2: Examples of each key type.

Sometimes a single attribute identifies an entity instance, such as **ISBN** for a title. When a single attribute makes up a key, we use the term *simple key*. A simple key can either be a business (also called natural) key or a surrogate key.

A business key is visible to the business (such as **Policy Number** for a **Policy**). A surrogate key is never visible to the business. A surrogate key is created by a technologist to help with a technology issue, such as space efficiency, speed, or integration. It is a unique identifier for a table, often a counter, usually fixed-size, and always system-generated without intelligence, so a surrogate key carries no business meaning.

Sometimes it takes more than one attribute to uniquely identify an entity instance. For example, both a **Promotion Type Code** and **Promotion Start Date** may be necessary to identify a promotion. When more than one attribute makes up a key, we use the term *compound key*. Therefore, **Promotion Type Code** and **Promotion Start Date** together are a compound candidate key for a promotion. When a key contains more than one piece of information, we use the term *composite key*. A simple key that includes the customer's first name, last name, and birthday, all in the same attribute, would be an example of a simple composite key. When a key contains different attributes, it is called an *overloaded* key. A **Student Grade** attribute might sometimes contain the actual grade, such as A, B, or C. At other times, it might contain a P for Pass and F for Fail. **Student Grade**, therefore, would be an overloaded attribute. **Student Grade** sometimes contains the student's grade, and other times indicates whether the student has passed the class.

Let's look at the model in Figure 26.

Figure 26: The entity on the many side contains a foreign key pointing back to the primary key from the entity on the one side.

Here are the rules captured on this model:

- Each **Gender** may categorize many **Pets**.
- Each **Pet** must be categorized by one **Gender**.
- Each **Pet** may Receive many **Vaccinations**.
- Each **Vaccination** may be given to many **Pets**.

The entity on the "one" side of the relationship is called the parent entity, and the entity on the "many" side of the relationship is called the child entity. For example, in the relationship between **Gender** and **Pet**, **Gender** is the parent and **Pet** is the child. When we create a relationship from a parent entity to a child entity, the parent's primary key is copied as a foreign key to the child. You can see the foreign key, **Gender Code**, in the **Pet** entity.

A foreign key is one or more attributes that link to another entity (or, in the case of a recursive relationship where two instances of the same entity may be related, that is, a relationship that starts and ends with the same entity, a link to the same entity). At the physical level, a foreign key allows a relational database management system to navigate from one table to another. For example, if we need to know the **Gender** of a particular **Pet**, we can use the **Gender Code** foreign key in **Pet** to navigate to the parent **Gender**.

Three model levels

Traditionally, data modeling produces a set of structures for a Relational Database Management System (RDBMS). First, we build the Conceptual Data Model (CDM) (more appropriately called the Business Terms Model or BTM for short) to capture the common business language for the initiative (e.g., "What's a Customer?"). Next, we create the Logical Data Model (LDM) using the BTM's common business language to precisely define the business requirements (e.g., "I need to see the customer's name and address on this report."). Finally, in the Physical Data Model (PDM), we design these business requirements specific for a particular technology such as Oracle, Teradata, or SQL Server (e.g., "Customer Last Name is a variable length not null field with a non-unique index..."). Our PDM represents the RDBMS design for an application. We then generate the Data Definition Language (DDL) from the PDM, which we can run within a RDBMS environment to create the set of tables that will store the application's data. To summarize, we go from common business language to business requirements to design to tables.

Although the conceptual, logical, and physical data models have played a very important role in application development over the last 50 years, they will play an even more important role over the next 50 years.

Regardless of the technology, data complexity, or breadth of requirements, there will always be a need for a diagram that captures the business language (conceptual), the business requirements (logical), and the design (physical).

The names *conceptual*, *logical*, and *physical*, however, are deeply rooted in the RDBMS side. Therefore, we need more encompassing names to accommodate both RDBMS and NoSQL for all three levels.

Align = Conceptual, Refine = Logical, Design = Physical

Using the terms Align, Refine, and Design instead of Conceptual, Logical, and Physical has two benefits: greater purpose and broader context.

Greater purpose means that by rebranding into Align, Refine, and Design, we include what the level does in the name. Align is about agreeing on the common business vocabulary so everyone is *aligned* on terminology and general initiative scope. Refine is about capturing the business requirements. That is, refining our knowledge of the initiative to focus on what is important. Design is about the technical requirements. That is, making sure we accommodate the unique needs of software and hardware on our model.

Broader context means there is more than just the models. When we use terms such as conceptual, most project teams only see the model as the deliverable, and do not recognize all of the work that went into producing the model or other related deliverables such as definitions, issue/question resolutions, and lineage (lineage meaning where the data comes from). The align phase includes the conceptual (business terms) model, the refine phase includes the logical model, and the design phase includes the physical model. We don't lose our modeling terms. Instead, we distinguish the model from its broader phase. For example, instead of saying we are in the logical data modeling phase, we say we are in the refine phase, where the logical data model is one of the deliverables. The logical data model exists within the context of the broader refine phase.

However, if you are working with a group of stakeholders who may not warm up to the traditional names of conceptual, logical, and physical, you can call the conceptual the *alignment model*, the logical the *refinement model*, and the physical the *design model*. Use the terms that would have the largest positive impact on your audience.

The conceptual level is Align, the logical Refine, and the physical Design. Align, Refine, and Design—easy to remember and even rhymes!

Business terms (Align)

We have had many experiences where people who need to speak a common business language do not consistently use the same set of terms. For example, Steve recently facilitated a discussion between a senior business analyst and a senior manager at a large insurance company.

The senior manager expressed his frustration on how a business analyst was slowing down the development of his business analytics application. "The team was meeting with the product owner and business users to complete the user stories on insurance quotes for our upcoming analytics application on quotes, when a business analyst asked the question, *What is a quote?* The rest of the meeting was wasted on trying to answer this question. Why couldn't we just focus on getting the Quote Analytics requirements, which we were in that meeting to do? We are supposed to be Agile!"

If there was a lengthy discussion trying to clarify the meaning of a quote, there is a good chance this insurance company does not understand a quote well. All business users may agree that a quote is an estimate for a policy premium but disagree at what point an estimate becomes a quote. For example, does an estimate have to be based on a certain percentage of facts before it can be considered a quote?

How well will Quote Analytics meet the user requirements if the users are not clear as to what a *quote* is? Imagine needing to know the answer to this question:

How many life insurance quotes were written last quarter in the northeast?

Without a common alignment and understanding of *quote,* one user can answer this question based on their definition of *quote,* and someone else can answer based on their different definition of *quote.* One of these users (or possibly both) will most likely get the wrong answer.

Steve worked with a university whose employees could not agree on what a *student* meant, a manufacturing company whose sales and accounting departments differed on the meaning of *return on total assets,* and a financial company whose analysts battled relentlessly over the meaning of a *trade*—it's all the same challenge we need to overcome, isn't it?

It's about working towards a common business language.

A common business language is a prerequisite for success in any initiative. We can capture and communicate the terms underlying business processes and requirements, enabling people with different backgrounds and roles to understand and communicate with each other.

A Conceptual Data Model (CDM), more appropriately called a Business Terms Model (BTM), is a language of symbols and text that simplifies an informational landscape by providing a precise, minimal, and visual tool scoped for a particular initiative and tailored for a particular audience.

This definition includes the need to be well-scoped, precise, minimal, and visual. Knowing the type of visual that will have the greatest effectiveness requires knowing the audience for the model.

The audience includes the people who will validate and use the model. Validate means telling us whether the model is correct or needs adjustments. Use means reading and benefiting from the model. The scope encompasses an initiative, such as an application development project or a business intelligence program.

Knowing the audience and scope helps us decide which terms to model, what the terms mean, how the terms relate to each other, and the most beneficial type of visual.

Additionally, knowing the scope ensures we don't "boil the ocean" and model every possible term in the enterprise. Instead, only focusing on those that will add value to our current initiative.

Although this model is traditionally called a *conceptual data model*, the term "conceptual" is often not received as a very positive term by those outside the data field. "Conceptual" sounds like a term the IT team would come up with. Therefore, we prefer to call the "conceptual data model" the "business terms model" and will use this term going forward. It is about business terms, and including the term "business" raises its importance as a business-focused deliverable and also aligns with data governance.

A business terms model often fits nicely on a single piece of paper—and not a plotter-size paper! Limiting a BTM to one page is important because it encourages us to select only key terms. We can fit 20 terms on one page but not 500 terms.

Being well-scoped, precise, minimal, and visual, the BTM provides a common business language. As a result, we can capture and communicate complex and encompassing business processes and requirements, enabling people with different backgrounds and roles to initially discuss and debate terms, and to eventually communicate effectively using these terms.

With more and more data being created and used, combined with intense competition, strict regulations, and rapid-spread social media, the financial, liability, and credibility stakes have never been higher. Therefore, the need for a common business language has never been greater. For example, Figure 27 contains a BTM for our animal shelter.

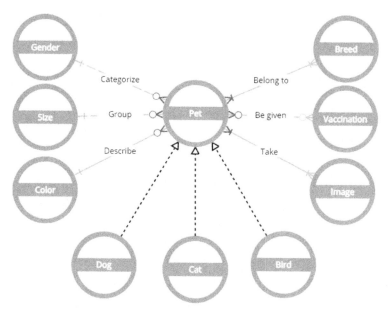

Figure 27: A business terms model for our animal shelter.

Each of these entities will have a precise and clear definition. For example, **Pet** might have a similar definition to what appears in Wikipedia:

A pet, or companion animal, is an animal kept primarily for a person's company or entertainment rather than as a working animal, livestock, or a laboratory animal.

More than likely, though, there will be something about the definition that provides more meaning to the reader of a particular data model and is more specific to a particular initiative, such as:

A pet is a dog, cat, or bird that has passed all the exams required to secure adoption. For example, if Sparky has passed all of his physical and behavioral exams, we would consider Sparky a pet. However, if Sparky has failed at least one exam, we will label Sparky an animal that we will reevaluate later.

Let's now walk through the relationships:

- Each Pet may be either a Dog, Cat, or Bird.
- Dog is a Pet.
- Cat is a Pet.
- Bird is a Pet.
- Each Gender may categorize many Pets.
- Each Pet must be categorized by one Gender.
- Each Size may group many Pets.
- Each Pet must be grouped by one Size.
- Each Color may describe many Pets.
- Each Pet must be described by one Color.
- Each Pet must belong to many Breeds.
- Each Breed may categorize many Pets.
- Each Pet may be given many Vaccinations.
- Each Vaccination may be given to many Pets.
- Each Pet must take many Images.
- Each Image must be taken of many Pets.

Logical (Refine)

A logical data model (LDM) is a business solution to a business problem. It is how the modeler refines the business requirements without complicating the model with implementation concerns such as software and hardware.

For example, after capturing the common business language for a new order application on a BTM, the LDM will refine this model with attributes and more detailed relationships and entities to capture the requirements for this order application. The BTM would contain definitions for **Order** and **Customer**, and the LDM would contain the **Order** and **Customer** attributes needed to deliver the requirements.

Returning to our animal shelter example, Figure 28 contains a subset of the logical data model for our animal shelter.

Figure 28: Logical data model subset for our animal shelter.

The requirements for our shelter application appear on this model. This model shows the attributes and relationships needed to deliver a solution to the business. For example, in the **Pet** entity, each **Pet** is identified by a **Pet Number** and described by its name and gender. **Gender** and **Vaccination** are defined lists. We also capture that a **Pet** must have one **Gender** and can receive any number (including zero) of **Vaccinations**.

Note that an LDM in the context of relational databases respects the rules of normalization. Hence, in the above diagram, there are associative entities, also known as "junction tables", which prepare for the physical implementation of many-to-many relationships.

Since Oracle duality views allow us to embed and denormalize, we often don't need these "junction tables" and opt for a simpler view of the same business rules. We can keep together what belongs together, following the Domain-Driven Design concept of "aggregates" discussed below, and leverage denormalization. See Figure 29.

Figure 29: This denormalized representation can easily lead to a normalized physical data model, whereas the opposite is not necessarily true in more complex configurations.

An important part of the requirements-gathering exercise is identifying, quantifying, and qualifying the workload by recording the frequency of queries, latency of results, volume and velocity of data, retentions, etc. We will cover this in more detail in the Refine chapter.

Domain-Driven Data Modeling

It is useful at this stage to discuss data modeling methodology, given that it has sometimes been accused of being in the way of getting things done. As stated in the Agile Manifesto's history page[3]: *We embrace modeling, but not in order to file some diagram in a dusty corporate repository.* We've all seen ER (Entity Relationship) diagrams so big that no one understands them anymore or dares to touch them for fear of breaking them. To address this concern, Hackolade has found inspiration in a popular software development methodology called *Domain-Driven Design* and applied some of its principles to data modeling.

Eric Evans is the author of the book, *Domain-Driven Design: Tackling Complexity in the Heart of Software*, published in 2003, considered one of the most influential works on Domain-Driven Design (DDD).

---

[3] https://agilemanifesto.org/history.html.

The principles of Domain-Driven Data Modeling[4] (DDDM) include:

- **Ubiquitous language**: establishing a common language used by all project stakeholders and reflecting the concepts and terms relevant to the business. A BTM helps build a common vocabulary. DDDM pushes further for developers to use this language in the code and in the name of collections/tables and fields/columns.

- **Bounded context**: managing the complexity of the system by breaking it down into smaller, more manageable pieces. We define a boundary around each specific domain of the system. Each bounded context has its own model and language that is appropriate for that context.

- **Focus on the core domain:** concentrating efforts for maximum impact on what matters most, without letting scope creep, and while leveraging pre-existing conformed dimensions and generic concepts.

---

[4] https://hackolade.com/dddm.html.

- **Reach a shared understanding**: collaborating with subject matter experts in the business to ensure alignment on the context and meaning of data.

- **Aggregates**: identifying clusters of related objects and treating each of them as a single unit of change. Aggregates help to enforce consistency and integrity within a domain.

- **Continuous refinement**: an iterative process with continuous refinement of the domain model as we discover new insights and requirements. The domain model should evolve and improve based on feedback from stakeholders and users.

Some data modeling traditionalists have expressed reservations about DDD (and also about Agile development.) For every methodology and technology, there are, of course, examples of misinterpretation and misguided efforts. However, if applied with clairvoyance and experience, DDDM and Agile lead to great success.

DDDM is particularly relevant in the context of NoSQL databases and modern architecture patterns, including event-driven[5] and micro-services.[6] Specifically, the DDDM

---

[5] https://en.wikipedia.org/wiki/Event-driven_architecture.

[6] https://en.wikipedia.org/wiki/Microservices.

concept of *aggregate* objects and denormalization. As a result, the strict definition of a logical data model is too constraining as it implies that the technology-agnostic model respects the rules of normalization. Hackolade has extended the capabilities of its technology-agnostic models to allow complex data types for nesting and denormalization in Polyglot data models to accommodate the support of NoSQL structures.

Physical (Design)

The Physical Data Model (PDM) is the logical data model compromised for specific software or hardware. The BTM captures our common business vocabulary, the LDM our business requirements, and the PDM our technical requirements. That is, the PDM is a data model of our business requirements structured to work well with our technology. The physical represents the technical design.

While building the PDM, we address the issues that have to do with specific hardware or software, such as, how can we best design our structures to:

- Process this operational data as quickly as possible?
- Make this information secure?
- Answer these business questions with a sub-second response?

For example, Figure 30 contains a relational version and Figure 31 a nested version of a subset of the physical data model for our animal shelter. Figure 30 is a normalized RDBMS model and Figure 31 shows one possible denormalization (JSON document) assembled and returned by an Oracle duality view.

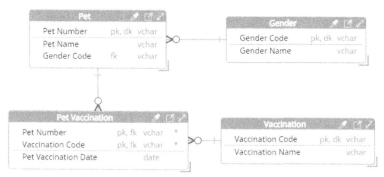

Figure 30: Relational physical data models for our animal shelter.

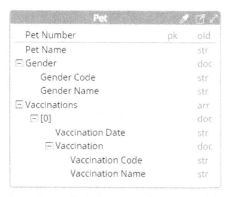

Figure 31: Nested physical data models for our animal shelter.

Information belonging together is kept together with the nesting of subobjects. The cardinality of the relational junction table Pet Vaccination is replaced by an array to store multiple Vaccinations. This aggregation approach ensures the referential integrity of the atomic unit of each document.

The document in Figure 31 shows that vaccinations are nested information for each pet. If we had an access pattern that needed direct access to vaccinations (independently of pets), we would just create another duality view. Oracle's duality views store the vaccinations in both document types. This differs from a pure NoSQL database, where we must synchronize different physical data models to ensure consistency.

Three model perspectives, plus a new one

Relational Database Management System (RDBMS) and NoSQL are the two main modeling perspectives. We include a combined perspective in Oracle Duality Views.

Within the RDBMS perspective, there are two settings: relational and dimensional. Within the NoSQL perspective, there is a single setting that we call "query", a more generic term that includes NoSQL. Therefore, the three modeling perspectives are relational, dimensional, and query. Oracle's JSON-relational duality combines the "relational" and "query" perspectives. Table 3 contrasts relational, dimensional, and query. In this section, we will go into more detail into each of these perspectives.

A RDBMS stores data in sets based on Ted Codd's groundbreaking research papers written from 1969 through 1974. Codd's ideas were implemented in the RDBMS with tables (entities at the physical level) containing attributes. Each table usually has primary key and foreign key constraints to enforce the relationships between tables.

Factor	Relational	Dimensional	Query
Benefit	Precisely representing data through sets	Precisely representing how data will be analyzed	Precisely representing how data will be received and accessed
Focus	Business rules *constraining* a business process	Business questions *analyzing* a business process	Access paths *providing* *insights* into a business process
Use case	Operational (OLTP)	Analytics (OLAP)	Discovery
Parent perspective	RDBMS	RDBMS	NoSQL
Example	A Customer must own at least one Account.	How much revenue did we generate in fees by Date, Region, and Product? Also want to see by Month and Year...	Which customers own a checking account that generated over $10,000 in fees this year, own at least one cat, and live within 500 miles of New York City?

Table 3: Comparing relational, dimensional, and query.

The RDBMS has been around for so many years primarily because of its ability to retain data integrity by enforcing rules that maintain high-quality data. Secondly, the RDBMS enables efficiency in storing data, reducing redundancy, preventing inconsistencies, and saving storage space. Over the last decade, the benefit of saving space has diminished, but avoiding inconsistencies and keeping update logic simple still remain important.

NoSQL means "NoRDBMS". A NoSQL database stores data differently than a RDBMS. An RDBMS stores data in tables (sets) where primary and foreign keys drive data integrity and navigation. A NoSQL database does not store data in sets. NoSQL solutions may store data in Resource Description Framework (RDF) triples, Extensible Markup Language (XML), or JavaScript Object Notation (JSON).

Relational, dimensional, and query can exist at all three model levels, giving us nine different types of models, as shown in Table 4. In the previous section, we discussed the three levels of Align, Refine, and Design. We align on a common business language, refine our business requirements, and then design our database. For example, if we are modeling a new claims application for an insurance company, we might create a relational model capturing the business rules within the claims process. The BTM would capture the claims business vocabulary, the LDM would capture the claims business requirements, and the PDM would capture the claims database design.

	RELATIONAL	DIMENSIONAL	NoSQL
BUSINESS TERMS (ALIGN)	TERMS AND RULES	TERMS AND PATHS	TERMS AND QUERIES
LOGICAL (REFINE)	SETS	MEASURES WITH CONTEXT	QUERY-FOCUSED HIERACHY
PHYSICAL (DESIGN)	COMPROMISED SETS	STAR SCHEMA OR SNOWFLAKE	ENHANCED HIERACHY

Table 4: Nine different types of models.

Relational

Relational models work best when there is a requirement to capture and enforce business rules. For example, a relational model may be ideal if an operational application requires applying many business rules, such as an order application ensuring that every order line belongs to one and only one order, and that each order line is identified by its order number plus a sequence number. The relational perspective focuses on business rules.

Relational models also excel if there are multiple access patterns or if different attributes of the data are selected or updated for different use cases. For example, private data like a salary should not be part of one use case (like an employee search in a company) but part of another (paycheck).

We can build a relational model at all three levels: business terms, logical, and physical. The relational business terms model contains the common business language for a particular initiative. Relationships capture the business rules between these terms. The relational logical data model includes entities along with their definitions, relationships, and attributes. The relational physical data model includes physical structures such as tables, columns, and constraints. The business terms, logical, and physical data models shared earlier are examples of relational. See Figure 32, Figure 33, and Figure 34.

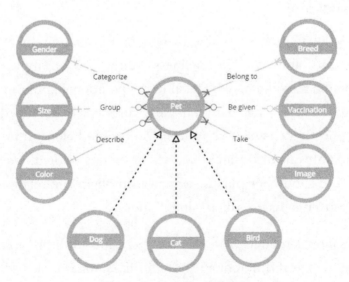

Figure 32: Relational BTM.

Figure 33: Relational LDM.

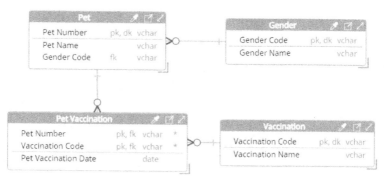

Figure 34: Relational PDM.

Figure 35 contains another example of a BTM.

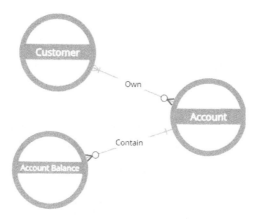

Figure 35: Relational BTM.

The relationships capture that:

- Each **Customer** may own many **Accounts**.
- Each **Account** must be owned by many **Customers**.
- Each **Account** may contain many **Account Balances**.
- Each **Account Balance** must belong to one **Account**.

We wrote the following definitions during one of our meetings with the project sponsor:

Customer	A customer is a person or organization who has opened one or more accounts with our bank. If members of a household each have their own account, each member of a household is considered a distinct customer. If someone has opened an account and then closed it, they are still considered a customer.
Account	An account is a contractual arrangement by which our bank holds funds on behalf of a customer.
Account Balance	An account balance is a financial record of how much money a customer has in a particular account with our bank at the end of a given time period, such as someone's checking account balance at the end of a month.

For the relational logical data model, we assign attributes to entities (sets) using a set of rules called *normalization*.

Although normalization has a foundation in mathematics (set theory and predicate calculus), we see it more as a technique to design a flexible structure. More specifically, we define normalization as a process of asking business questions, increasing your knowledge of the business and enabling you to build flexible structures that support high-quality data.

The business questions are organized around levels, including First Normal Form (1NF), Second Normal Form (2NF), and Third Normal Form (3NF). William Kent has neatly summarized these three levels:

Every attribute depends upon the key, the whole key, and nothing but the key, so help me Codd.

"Every attribute depends upon the key" is 1NF, "the whole key" is 2NF, and "nothing but the key" is 3NF. Note that the higher levels of normalization include the lower levels, so 2NF includes 1NF, and 3NF includes 2NF and 1NF.

To make sure that every attribute depends upon the key (1NF), we need to make sure for a given primary key value, we get at most one value back from each attribute. For example, **Author Name** assigned to a **Book** entity would violate 1NF because we can have more than author for a given book, such as this book. Therefore **Author Name** does not belong to the **Book** set (entity) and needs to be moved to a different entity. More than likely, **Author Name** will be assigned to the **Author** entity, and a relationship will exist between **Book** and **Author,** stating among other things, that a **Book** can be written by more than one **Author**.

To make sure every attribute depends upon the whole key (2NF), we need to make sure we have the minimal primary key. For example, if the primary key for **Book** was both **ISBN** and a **Book Title**, we would quickly learn that **Book Title** is not necessary to have in the primary key. An attribute such as **Book Price** would depend directly on the **ISBN,** and therefore, including **Book Title** in the primary key would not add any value.

To make sure there are no hidden dependencies ("nothing but the key," which is 3NF), we need to make sure every attribute depends directly on the primary key and nothing else. For example, the attribute **Order Gross Amount** does not depend directly on the primary key of **Order** (most likely, **Order Number**). Instead, **Order Gross Amount** depends upon **List Price** and **Item Quantity,** which derive the **Order Gross Amount**.

Data Modeling Made Simple, by Steve Hoberman, goes into more detail on each of the levels of normalization, including the levels above 3NF. Realize the main purpose of normalization is to correctly organize attributes into sets. Also, note that the normalized model is built according to the properties of the data and not built according to how the data is being used.

Dimensional models are built to answer specific business questions with ease, and NoSQL models are built to answer queries and identify patterns with ease. The relational is the only model focused on the intrinsic properties of the data and not usage.

Dimensional

A dimensional data model captures the business *questions* behind one or more business processes. The answers to the questions are metrics, such as **Gross Sales Amount** and **Customer Count**.

A dimensional model is a data model whose only purpose is to allow efficient and user-friendly filtering, sorting, and summing of measures. That is, analytics applications. The relationships on a dimensional model represent navigation paths instead of business rules, as with the relational model. The scope of a dimensional model is a collection of related measures plus context that together address some business process. We build dimensional models based upon one or more business questions that evaluate a business process. We parse the business questions into measures and ways of looking at these measures to create the model.

For example, suppose we work for a bank and would like to better understand the fee generation process. In that case, we might ask the business question, "What is the total amount of fees received by **Account Type** (such as Checking or Savings), **Month**, **Customer Category** (such as Individual or Corporate), and **Branch**?" See Figure 36. This model also communicates the requirement to see fees not just at a **Month** level but also at a **Year** level, not just a **Branch** level, but also at a **Region** and **District** level.

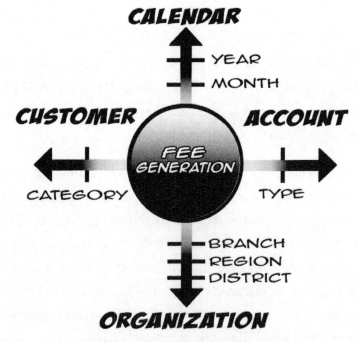

Figure 36: A dimensional BTM for a bank.

Term definitions:

Fee Generation	Fee generation is the business process where money is charged to customers for the privilege to conduct transactions against their account, or money charged based on time intervals, such as monthly charges to keep a checking account open that has a low balance.
Branch	A branch is a physical location open for business. Customers visit branches to conduct transactions.
Region	A region is our bank's own definition of dividing a country into smaller pieces for branch assignment or reporting purposes.
District	A district is a grouping of regions used for organizational assignments or reporting purposes. Districts can and often do cross country boundaries, such as North America and Europe districts.
Customer Category	A customer category is a grouping of one or more customers for reporting or organizational purposes. Examples of customer categories are Individual, Corporate, and Joint.
Account Type	An account type is a grouping of one or more accounts for reporting or organizational purposes. Examples of account types are Checking, Savings, and Brokerage.
Year	A year is a period of time containing 365 days, consistent with the Gregorian calendar.
Month	A month is each of the twelve named periods into which a year is divided.

You might encounter terms such as **Year** and **Month** which are commonly understood terms, and therefore minimal time can be invested in writing a definition. Make sure, though, that these are commonly understood terms, as sometimes even **Year** can have multiple meanings, such as whether the reference is to a fiscal or standard calendar.

Fee Generation is an example of a meter. A meter represents the business process that we need to measure. The meter is so important to the dimensional model that the name of the meter is often the name of the application: the **Sales** meter, the Sales Analytics Application. **District, Region**, and **Branch** represent the levels of detail we can navigate within the **Organization** dimension. A *dimension* is a subject whose purpose is to add meaning to the measures. For example, **Year** and **Month** represent the levels of detail we can navigate within the **Calendar** dimension. So this model contains four dimensions: **Organization, Calendar, Customer**, and **Account**.

Suppose an organization builds an analytical application to answer questions on how a business process is performing, such as a sales analytics application. Business questions become very important in this case, so we build a dimensional data model. The dimensional perspective focuses on business questions. We can build a dimensional data model at all three levels: business terms, logical, and physical. Figure 36 displays our business terms model, Figure 37 shows the logical, and Figure 38 the physical.

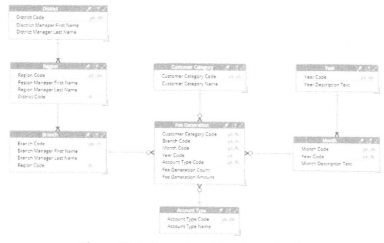

Figure 37: A dimensional LDM for a bank.

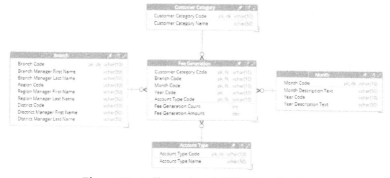

Figure 38: A dimensional PDM for a bank.

Query

Suppose an organization builds an application to discover something new about a business process, such as a fraud detection application. Queries become very important in that case, so we build a query data model.

We can build a query data model at all three levels: business terms, logical, and physical. Figure 39 contains a query business terms model, Figure 40 and Figure 41 the query logical data models, and Figure 42 the query physical data model.

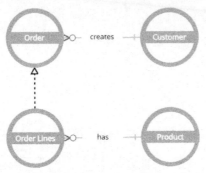

Figure 39: A query BTM.

The Query BTM does not look any different from other BTMs as the vocabulary and scope are the same, independent of the physical database implementation. In fact, we can even ask the Participation and Existence questions for each relationship in our query BTM, if we feel that it would add value. In the above example:

- a **Customer** creates an **Order**
- an **Order** is made of **Order Lines**
- an **Order Line** has a **Product**

It is possible to toggle the display of attributes for the different entities.

When it comes to the logical model, however, access patterns and workload analysis dictate the model.

Depending on whether there are queries for maintenance screens for Customers and Products, you could have the strictly embedded logical model in Figure 40 or the model in Figure 41.

Figure 40: Strictly embedded logical model.

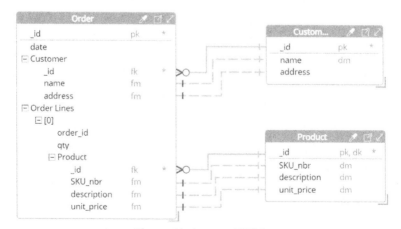

Figure 41: A query LDM.

The first logical model would lead to a single view in Oracle duality views, whereas it will be automatically normalized into three tables when instantiated to a physical model for a relational database.

The second logical model will lead to three Oracle duality views to accommodate the maintenance of **Customers** and **Products**, but keeping the **Order** table as an aggregate combines embedding and referencing schema design patterns.

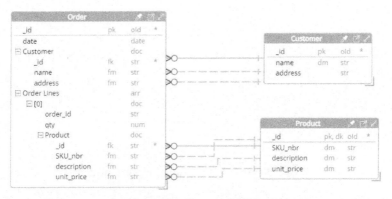

Figure 42: A query PDM.

In the above model, we show nesting, denormalization, and referencing. Nesting allows aggregating information that belongs together in a user-friendly structure to make it easily understandable by humans. Denormalization is implemented so a query to retrieve an order would fetch all of the necessary information in a single seek, without having to execute expensive joins, even if it is a repetition of the data in the master collections Customer and Product.

Access patterns might still be required to view and update Customer and Product information regardless of the orders to which they might be linked. Therefore, we keep the master Customer collection and the master Product collection. In the Order collection, we keep a reference to the master document. Since no cross-document referential integrity is built into the database engine, the responsibility to maintain the synchronization shifts to the application or to an offline process such as a Kafka pub/sub pipeline.

There could be a good reason to not update a denormalized piece of information. For example, the ship-to address of an already fulfilled order should not be updated because a customer moves to a new address. Only pending orders should be updated. Denormalization is sometimes more precise than cascading updates.

JSON-relational duality

Oracle's new paradigm, *JSON-relational duality*, aims to make the choice between the relational and query (JSON) models obsolete. Conceptually, a developer uses both models simultaneously while the Oracle database takes care of the underlying consistent storage and efficient execution of queries and DML (updates, inserts, deletes).

For JSON-relational duality, it is still important to understand data normalization as different levels of normalization are possible. When we normalize to the fullest extent, every scalar value in a JSON document maps to a column in a table. Substructures, like arrays, would usually map to another table that needs to be joined to assemble the JSON document. This can be a desired feature if the nested structure is shared with other documents or independent access to the table is required.

Let's look at an example: an order belongs to one customer, but a customer may have multiple addresses. With classic relational normalization, there would be an 'address' table that is separate from the 'customer' table because there is a one-to-many relationship between both (if a customer was only allowed to have one address, we could merge the attributes of address and customer).

The fact that 'address' requires a separate table is a consequence of the cardinality of the relationship. It does not mean that we want to use an address independently of a customer. This is important to understand as JSON Duality Views offer a choice here.

A table in an Oracle database can contain one or even multiple JSON type columns. It would be possible to store an array of addresses inside a JSON column of the customer table, therefore obsoleting the need for a separate address table (and a join).

One way to describe a relationship is whether it's an 'owning relationship' or 'reference relationship'. These are not official terms, but they help to understand the nature of how two entities are related to each other. Intuitively, we could say that an order refers to a customer because other orders (or even other entities) could point to the same customer. On the other hand, the address is 'owned' by the customer and no other customer will have to point to the same address.

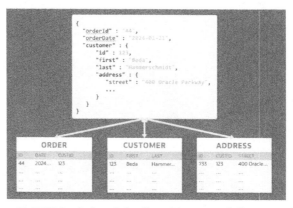

Figure 43: JSON-relational duality object over fully normalized tables.

The fact that a relational table cannot only contain scalar SQL columns (like number, string, date) but also JSON to store entire structures allow totally new ways to design a schema and to combine relational strengths (independent entities) with the strength of NoSQL databases (avoiding joins, schema flexibility, polymorphism).

JSON-relational duality Views generate JSON objects from data in tables, columns, and rows. A JSON type column's value will be merged naturally into the JSON such that nobody can tell from looking at a document returned by a duality document whether a value came from a relational column or a JSON type column.

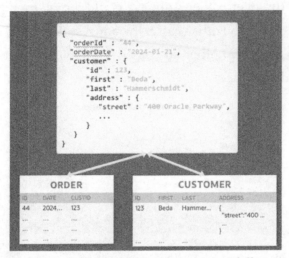

Figure 44: JSON-relational duality object over partially normalized tables using a JSON column to store a nested structure.

JSON-Relational Duality views do not have to select all columns in a table; instead, they select the relevant columns for a given use case. It is possible to have multiple views over the same tables selecting different or overlapping columns. One benefit of this flexibility is that it is easy to omit columns or data that should be hidden from an application for privacy or security reasons. For example, it would be easy to have 3 views for 'employees': one that shows all attributes but hides the salary, another one that shows the salary but does not allow updates, and one that shows the salary and allows to update it.

CHAPTER 1

Align

This chapter will explain the data modeling align phase. We explain the purpose of aligning our business vocabulary, introduce our animal shelter case study, and then walk through the align approach. We end this chapter with three tips and three takeaways.

Purpose

The align stage aims to capture a common business vocabulary within a business terms model for a particular initiative.

For NoSQL models, you might use a different term than a business terms model, such as a *query alignment model*. We also like this term, which is more specific to the purpose of a NoSQL BTM, as our goal is modeling the queries.

Our animal shelter

A small animal shelter needs our help. They currently advertise their ready-to-adopt pets on their own website. They use a Microsoft Access relational database to keep track of their animals, and they publish this data weekly on their website. See Figure 45 for their current process.

A Microsoft Access record is created for each animal after the animal passes a series of intake tests and is deemed ready for adoption. The animal is called a pet once they are ready for adoption.

Once a week, the pet records are updated on the shelter's website. New pets are added and adopted pets have been removed.

Figure 45: Animal shelter current architecture.

Not many people know about this shelter, and, therefore, animals often remain unadopted for much longer than the national average. Consequently, they would like to partner with a group of animal shelters to form a consortium where all of the shelters' pet information will appear on a much more popular website. Our shelter will need to extract data from its current MS Access database and send it to the consortium database in JSON format. The consortium will then load these JSON feeds into their Oracle duality views with a web front end.

Let's now look at the shelter's current models.

The animal shelter built the business terms model (BTM) in Figure 46 to capture the common business language for the initiative.

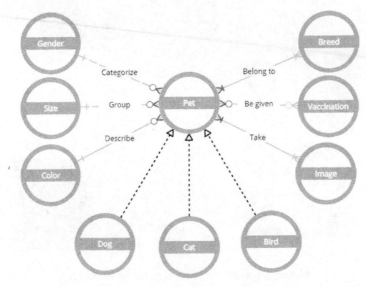

Figure 46: Animal shelter BTM.

In addition to this diagram, the BTM also contains precise definitions for each term, such as this definition **Pet** mentioned earlier in the chapter:

A pet is a dog, cat, or bird that has passed all the exams required to secure adoption. For example, if Sparky has passed all of his physical and behavioral exams, we would consider Sparky a pet. However, if Sparky has failed at least one exam, we will label Sparky an animal that we will reevaluate later.

Our animal shelter knows its world well and has built fairly solid models. Recall they will send a subset of their data to a consortium via JSON, which the consortium's Oracle duality views database will receive and load for display on their website. Let's go through the align, refine, and design approach for the consortium, and then work on the JSON structure required to move the shelter's data from Microsoft Access to Oracle duality views.

Approach

The align stage is about developing the initiative's common business vocabulary. We will follow the steps shown in Figure 47.

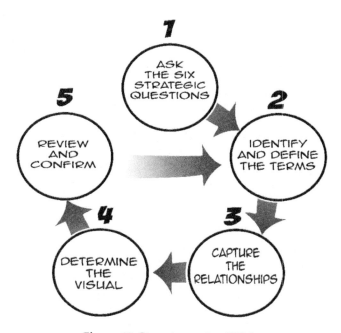

Figure 47: Steps to create a BTM.

Before you begin any project, we must ask six strategic questions (Step 1). These questions are a prerequisite to the success of any initiative because they ensure we choose the right terms for our BTM. Next, identify all terms within the scope of the initiative (Step 2). Make sure each term is clearly and completely defined. Then, determine how these terms relate to each other (Step 3). Often, you will need to go back to Step 2 at this point because in capturing relationships, you may come up with new terms. Next, determine the most beneficial visual for your audience (Step 4). Consider the visual that would resonate best with those needing to review and use your BTM. As a final step, seek approval of your BTM (Step 5). At this point, there are often additional changes to the model, and we cycle through these steps until the model is accepted.

Let's build a BTM following these five steps.

Step 1: Ask the six strategic questions

We need to ask six questions to ensure a valuable BTM. These questions appear in Figure 48.

1. **What is our initiative?** This question ensures we know enough about the initiative to determine the scope. Knowing the scope allows us to decide which terms should appear on the initiative's BTM. In his book Domain-Driven Design, Eric Evans

introduces the concept of "Bounded Context," which is all about understanding and defining your scope. For example, terms such as **Animal**, **Shelter Employee**, and **Pet Food** are out of scope.

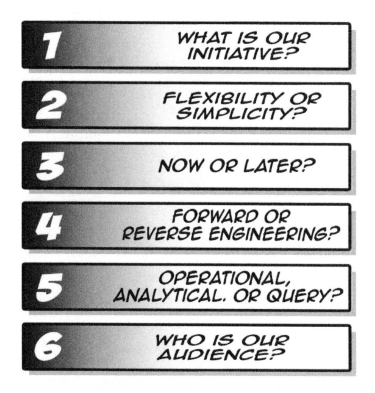

Figure 48: Six questions to ensure model success.

2. **Flexibility or simplicity?** This question ensures we introduce generic terms only if there is a need for flexibility. Generic terms allow us to accommodate new types of terms that we do not know about today and also allow us to better group similar terms together. For example, **Person** is flexible and

Employee is simple. **Person** can include other terms we have not yet considered, such as **Adopter, Veterinarian**, and **Volunteer**. However, **Person** can be a more difficult term to relate to than **Employee.** We often describe our processes using business-specific terms like **Employee.**

3. **Now or later?** This question ensures we have chosen the correct time perspective for our BTM. BTMs capture a common business language at a point in time. If we are intent on capturing how business processes work or are analyzed today, then we need to make sure terms, along with their definitions and relationships, reflect a current perspective (now). If we are intent on capturing how business processes work or are analyzed at some point in the future, such as one year or three years into the future, then we need to make sure terms, along with their definitions and relationships, reflect a future perspective (later).

4. **Forward or reverse engineering?** This question ensures we select the most appropriate "language" for the BTM. If business requirements drive the initiative, then it is a forward engineering effort and we choose a business language. It does not matter whether the organization is using SAP or Siebel, the BTM will contain business terms. If an application is driving the initiative, then it is a

reverse engineering effort and we choose an application language. If the application uses the term **Object** for the term **Product**, it will appear as **Object** on the model and be defined according to how the application defines the term, not how the business defines the term. As another example of reverse engineering, you might have some type of physical data structure as your starting point, such as a database layout, XML, or JSON document. For example, the following JSON snippet might reveal the importance of **Shelter Volunteer** as a business term:

```
{
  "name": "John Smith",
  "age": 35,
  "address": {
    "street": "123 Main St",
    "city": "Anytown",
    "state": "CA",
    "zip": "12345"
  }
}
```

5. **Operational, analytics, or query?** This question ensures we choose the right type of BTM—relational, dimensional, or query. Each initiative requires its respective BTM.

6. **Who is our audience?** We need to know who will review our model (validator) and who will use our model going forward (users).

1. What is our initiative?

Mary is the animal shelter volunteer responsible for intake. Intake is the process of receiving an animal and preparing the animal for adoption. She has been a volunteer for over ten years, and was the main business resource in building the original Microsoft Access database.

She is enthusiastic about the new initiative, seeing it as a way to get animals adopted in less time. We might start off by interviewing Mary, where the goal is to have a clear understanding of the initiative, including its scope:

> **You**: Thanks for making time to meet with me. This is just our first meeting, and I don't want to keep you behind our allocated time, so let's get right to the purpose of our interview and then a few questions. The earlier we identify our scope and then define the terms within this scope, the greater the chance for success. Can you please share with me more about this initiative?

> **Mary**: Sure! The main driver for our initiative is to make our furry friends get adopted faster. Today on average, our pets are adopted in two weeks. We and other small local shelters would like to get this down to five days on average. Maybe even less, hope so. We will send our pet data to a consortium we have formed with other local shelters to centralize our listings and reach a wider audience.

> **You**: Do you have all types of pets, or just dogs and cats?

Mary: I'm not sure what kinds of pets the other shelters have other than dogs and cats, but we also have birds up for adoption.

You: Ok, and are there any pets to exclude from this initiative?

Mary: Well, it takes a few days for an animal to be assessed to be considered ready for adoption. We run some tests and sometimes procedures. I like to use the term pet when an animal has completed these processes and is now ready for adoption. So we do have animals that are not yet pets. We are only including pets in this initiative.

You: Got it. And when somebody is looking for a furry best friend, what kinds of filters would they use?

Mary: I've talked with volunteers at the other shelters too. We feel after filtering first on the type of pet, such as dog, cat, or bird, filtering by breed, gender, color, and size would be the most important filters.

You: What kinds of information would someone expect to see when clicking on a pet description that was returned by the filter selections?

Mary: Lots of images, a cute name, maybe information on the pet's color or breed. That sort of thing.

You: Makes sense. What about people? Do you care about people as part of this initiative?

Mary: What do you mean?

You: Well, the people who drop off pets and the people who adopt pets.

Mary: Yes, yes. We keep track of this information. By the way, the people who drop off animals we call surrenderers, and the people who adopt pets are adopters. We are not sending any person details to the consortium. We don't see it relevant and don't want to risk getting sued over privacy issues. Spot the dog will never sue us, but Bob the surrenderer might.

You: I can understand that. Well, I think I understand the scope of the initiative, thank you.

We now have a good understanding of the scope of the initiative. It includes all pets (not all animals) and no people. As we refine the terminology, we might have more questions for Mary around scope.

2. Flexibility or simplicity?

Let's continue the interview to answer the next question.

You: Flexibility or simplicity?

Mary: I don't understand the question.

You: We need to determine whether to use generic terms or, for lack of a better word, more concrete terms. Using generic terms, such as mammal instead of **dog** or **cat**, allows us to accommodate future terms later, such as other kinds of mammals like monkeys or whales.

Mary: We haven't had many whales up for adoption this month. [laughs]

You: Ha!

Mary: Flexibility sounds appealing, but we shouldn't go overboard. I can see that, eventually, we might have other kinds of pets, so a certain level of flexibility would be useful here. But not too much. I remember working on the Microsoft Access system and someone was trying to get us to use a Party concept to capture dogs and cats. It was too hard for us to get our heads around it. Too fuzzy, if you know what I mean.

You: I do know what you mean. Ok, a little flexibility to accommodate different kinds of pets, but not to go overboard. Got it.

3. Now or later?

Now on to the next question.

You: Should our model reflect how things are now at the shelter or how you would like it to be after the consortium's application is live?

Mary: I don't think it matters. We are not changing anything with the new system. A pet is a pet.

You: Ok, that makes things easy.

As we can see from our conversations on these first three questions, getting to the answers is rarely straightforward and easy. However, it is much more efficient to ask them at the beginning of the initiative instead of making assumptions early on and having to perform rework later, when changes are time-consuming and expensive.

4. Forward or reverse engineering?

Since we first need to understand how the business works before implementing a software solution, this is a forward engineering project, and we will choose the forward engineering option. This means that we are driven by requirements, and therefore, our terms will be business terms instead of application terms.

5. Operational, analytics, or query?

Since this initiative is about displaying pet information to drive pet adoption, which is query, we will build a query BTM.

6. Who is our audience?

That is, who is going to validate the model and who is going to use it going forward? Mary seems like the best candidate to be the validator. She knows the existing application and processes very well and is vested in ensuring the new initiative succeeds. Potential adopters will be the users of the system.

Step 2: Identify and define the terms

We first focus on the user stories, then determine the detailed queries for each story, and finally sequence these queries in the order they occur. It can be iterative. For example, we might identify the sequence between two queries and realize that a query in the middle is missing that will require modifying or adding a user story. Let's go through each of these three steps.

1. Write user stories

User stories have been around for a long time and are extremely useful for NoSQL modeling. Wikipedia defines a user story as: *...an informal, natural language description of features of a software system.*

The user story provides the scope and overview for the BTM, also known as a query alignment model. A query alignment model accommodates one or more user stories. The purpose of a user story is to capture at a very high level how an initiative will deliver business value. User stories take the structure of the template in Figure 49.

TEMPLATE	COVERS
AS A (STAKEHOLDER)	WHO?
I WANT TO (REQUIREMENT)	WHAT?
SO THAT (MOTIVATION)	WHY?

Figure 49: User story template.

Here are some examples of user stories from tech.gsa.gov:

- As a Content Owner, I want to be able to create product content so that I can provide information and market to customers.

- As an Editor, I want to review content before it is published so that I can ensure it is optimized with correct grammar and tone.

- As a HR Manager, I need to view a candidate's status so that I can manage their application process throughout the recruiting phases.

- As a Marketing Data Analyst, I need to run the Salesforce and Google analytics reports so that I can build the monthly media campaign plans.

To keep our animal shelter example relatively simple, assume our animal shelter and others that are part of the consortium met and determined these are the most popular user stories:

1. As a potential dog adopter, I want to find a particular breed, color, size, and gender, so that I get the type of dog I am looking. I want to ensure that the dog's vaccinations are up-to-date.

2. As a potential bird adopter, I want to find a particular breed and color so that I get the bird I am looking for.

3. As a potential cat adopter, I want to find a particular color and gender, so that I get the type of cat I am looking for.

2. Capture queries

Next, we capture the queries for the one or more user stories within our initiative's scope. While we want to capture multiple user stories to ensure we have a firm grasp of the scope, having just a single user story that drives a NoSQL application is ok. A query starts off with a "verb" and is an action to do something. Some NoSQL database vendors use the phrase "access pattern" instead of query. We will use the term "query" to also encompass "access pattern".

Here are the queries that satisfy our three user stories:

Q1: Only show pets available for adoption.

Q2: Search available dogs by breed, color, size, and gender that have up-to-date vaccinations.

Q3: Search available birds by breed and color.

Q4: Search available cats by color and gender.

Now that we have direction, we can work with the business experts to identify and define the terms within the initiative's scope.

Recall our definition of a term as a noun that represents a collection of business data and is considered both basic and critical to your audience for a particular initiative. A term can fit into one of six categories: who, what, when, where, why, or how. We can use these six categories to create a terms template for capturing the terms on our BTM. See Figure 50.

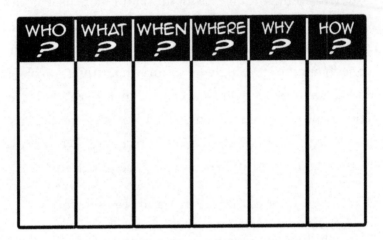

Figure 50: Terms template.

This is a handy brainstorming tool. There is no significance to the numbers. That is, a term written next to #1 is not meant to be more important than a term written next to #2. In addition, you can have more than five terms in a given column, or in some cases, no terms in a given column.

We meet again with Mary, and came up with this completed template in Figure 51, based on our queries.

WHO?	WHAT?	WHEN?	WHERE?	WHY?	HOW?
SURRENDERER	PET	VACCINATION DATE	CRATE	VACCINATE	VACCINATION
ADOPTER	DOG			ADOPT	ADOPTION
	CAT			PROMOTE	PROMOTION
	BIRD				
	BREED				
	GENDER				
	COLOR				
	SIZE				
	IMAGE				

Figure 51: Initially completed template for our animal shelter.

Notice that this is a brainstorming session, and terms might appear on this template but not on the relational BTM. Excluded terms fit into three categories:

- **Too detailed**. Attributes will appear on the LDM and not the BTM. For example, **Vaccination Date** is more detailed than **Pet** and **Breed**.

- **Out of scope**. Brainstorming is a great way to test the scope of the initiative. Often, terms added to the terms template require additional discussions to determine whether they are in scope. For example, **Surrenderer** and **Adopter** we know are out of scope for the animal shelter's initiative.

- **Redundancies**. Why and How can be very similar. For example, the event **Vaccinate** is documented by the **Vaccination**. The event **Adopt** is documented by **Adoption**. Therefore, we may not need both the event and documentation. In this case, we choose the documentation. That is, we choose How instead of Why.

After taking a lunch break, we met again with Mary and refined our terms template, as shown in Figure 52.

WHO ?	WHAT ?	WHEN ?	WHERE ?	WHY ?	HOW ?
~~SURRENDERER~~	PET	~~VACCINATION DATE~~	~~CRATE~~	~~VACCINATE~~	VACCINATION
~~ADOPTER~~	DOG			~~ADOPT~~	~~ADOPTION~~
	CAT			~~PROMOTE~~	~~PROMOTION~~
	BIRD				
	BREED				
	GENDER				
	COLOR				
	SIZE				
	IMAGE				

Figure 52: Refined template for our animal shelter.

We might have a lot of questions during this brainstorming session. It is a great idea to ask questions as they come up. There are three benefits of raising questions:

- **Become known as the detective**. Become comfortable with the level of detective work needed to arrive at a precise set of terms. Look for holes in the definition where ambiguity can sneak in, and ask questions the answers to which will make the definition precise. Consider the question, "Can a pet be of more than one breed?" The answer to this question will refine how the consortium views pets, breeds, and their relationship. A skilled detective remains pragmatic as well, careful to avoid "analysis paralysis". A skilled data modeler must also be pragmatic to ensure the delivery of value to the project team.

- **Uncover hidden terms**. The answers to questions often lead to more terms on our BTM—terms that we might have missed otherwise. For example, better understanding the relationship between **Vaccination** and **Pet** might lead to more terms on our BTM.

- **Better now than later**. The resulting BTM offers a lot of value, yet the process of getting to that final model is also valuable. Debates and questions challenge people, make them rethink, and, in some cases, defend their perspectives. If questions are not raised and answered during the process of building the BTM, the questions will be raised and need to be addressed later on in the lifecycle of the initiative, often in the form of data and process surprises, when changes are time-consuming and expensive. Even simple questions like "Are there other attributes that we could use to describe a pet?" can lead to a healthy debate resulting in a more precise BTM.

Here are definitions for each term:

Pet	A dog, cat, or bird that is ready and available to be adopted. An animal becomes a pet after they have passed certain exams administered by our shelter staff.
Gender	The biological sex of the pet. There are three values that we use at the shelter: • Male • Female • Unknown The unknown value is when we are unsure of the gender.
Size	The size is most relevant for dogs, and there are three values that we assign at the shelter: • Small • Medium • Large Cats and birds are assigned medium, except for kittens which are assigned small and parrots which are large.
Color	The primary shade of the pet's fur, feathers, or coat. Examples of colors include brown, red, gold, cream, and black. If a pet has multiple colors, we either assign a primary color or assign a more general term to encompass multiple colors, such as textured, spotted, or patched.
Breed	From Wikipedia, because this definition applies to our initiative: *A breed is a specific group of domestic animals having homogeneous appearance, homogeneous behavior, and/or other characteristics that distinguish it from other organisms of the same species.*

Vaccina-tion	A shot given to a pet to protect it from disease. Examples of vaccinations are rabies for dogs and cats, and polyomavirus vaccine for birds.
Image	A photograph taken of the pet that will be posted on the website.
Dog	From Wikipedia, because this definition applies to our initiative: *The dog is a domesticated descendant of the wolf. Also called the domestic dog, it is derived from the extinct Pleistocene wolf, and the modern wolf is the dog's nearest living relative. Dogs were the first species to be domesticated by hunter-gatherers over 15,000 years ago before the development of agriculture.*
Cat	From Wikipedia, because this definition applies to our initiative: *The cat is a domestic species of small carnivorous mammal. It is the only domesticated species in the family Felidae and is commonly referred to as the domestic cat or house cat to distinguish it from the wild members of the family.*
Bird	From Wikipedia, because this definition applies to our initiative: *Birds are a group of warm-blooded vertebrates constituting the class Aves, characterized by feathers, toothless beaked jaws, the laying of hard-shelled eggs, a high metabolic rate, a four-chambered heart, and a strong yet lightweight skeleton.*

Step 3: Capture the relationships

Even though this is a query BTM, we can ask the Participation and Existence questions to precisely display the business rules for each relationship. Participation questions determine whether there is a one or a many symbol on the relationship line next to each term. Existence questions determine whether there is a zero (may) or one (must) symbol on the relationship line next to either term.

Working with Mary, we identify these relationships on the model:

- **Pet** can be a **Bird, Cat,** or **Dog.** (Subtyping)
- **Pet** and **Image.**
- **Pet** and **Breed.**
- **Pet** and **Gender.**
- **Pet** and **Color.**
- **Pet** and **Vaccination.**
- **Pet** and **Size.**

Table 5 contains the answers to the Participation and Existence questions for each of these seven relationships (excluding the subtyping relationship). After translating the answer to each question into the model, we have the animal shelter BTM in Figure 53.

Question	Yes	No
Can a Gender categorize more than one Pet?	✓	
Can a Pet be categorized by more than one Gender?		✓
Can a Gender exist without a Pet?	✓	
Can a Pet exist without a Gender?		✓
Can a Size categorize more than one Pet?	✓	
Can a Pet be categorized by more than one Size?		✓
Can a Size exist without a Pet?	✓	
Can a Pet exist without a Size?		✓
Can a Color describe more than one Pet?	✓	
Can a Pet be described by more than one Color?		✓

Question	Yes	No
Can a Color exist without a Pet?	✓	
Can a Pet exist without a Color?		✓
Can a Pet be described by more than one Breed?	✓	
Can a Breed describe more than one Pet?	✓	
Can a Pet exist without a Breed?		✓
Can a Breed exist without a Pet?	✓	
Can a Pet be given more than one Vaccination?	✓	
Can a Vaccination be given to more than one Pet?	✓	
Can a Pet exist without a Vaccination?	✓	
Can a Vaccination exist without a Pet?	✓	
Can a Pet take more than one Image?	✓	
Can an Image be taken of more than one Pet?	✓	
Can a Pet exist without an Image?		✓
Can an Image exist without a Pet?		✓

Table 5: Answers to the Participation and Existence questions.

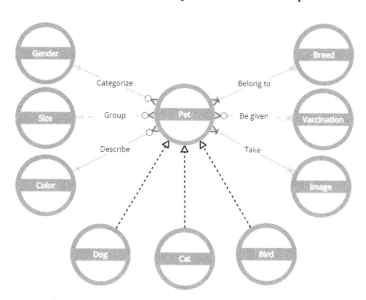

Figure 53: Our animal shelter BTM (showing rules).

These relationships are read as:

- Each **Gender** may categorize many **Pets**.
- Each **Pet** must be categorized by one **Gender**.
- Each **Size** may group many **Pets**.
- Each **Pet** must be grouped by one **Size**.
- Each **Color** may describe many **Pets**.
- Each **Pet** must be described by one **Color**.
- Each **Pet** must belong to many **Breeds**.
- Each **Breed** may be assigned to many **Pets**.
- Each **Pet** may be given many **Vaccinations**.
- Each **Vaccination** may be given to many **Pets**.
- Each **Pet** must take many **Images**.
- Each **Image** must be taken of many **Pets**.
- Each **Pet** may either be a **Dog**, **Cat**, or **Bird**.
- **Dog** is a **Pet**. **Cat** is a **Pet**. **Bird** is a **Pet**.

The answers to the participation and existence questions are context-dependent. That is, the scope of the initiative determines the answers. In this case, because our scope is the subset of the animal shelter's business that will be used as part of this consortium's project, we know at this point that a **Pet** must be described by only one **Color**.

We determined that Oracle duality views should be used to answer these queries. You can see how the traditional data model provides value by making us ask the right questions and then providing a powerful communication medium showing the terms and their business rules. Even if we are not implementing our solution in a relational database, this BTM provides value.

Build a relational data model even though the solution is Oracle duality views. If you feel there is value in explaining the terms with precision along with their business rules, build the relational BTM. If you feel there is value in organizing the attributes into sets using normalization, build the relational LDM. It will help you organize your thoughts and provide you with a very effective communication tool.

Our end goal, though, is to create Oracle duality views. Therefore, we need a query BTM. So, we need to determine the order in which someone would run the queries.

Graphing the sequence of queries leads to the query BTM. The query BTM is a numbered list of all queries necessary to deliver the user stories within the initiative's scope. The model also shows a sequence or dependency among the queries. The query BTM for our five queries would look like what appears in Figure 54.

All of the queries depend on the first query. That is, we first need to filter by animal type.

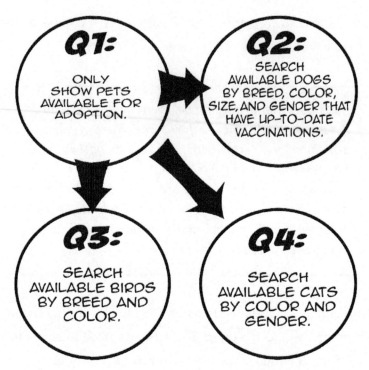

Figure 54: Our animal shelter BTM (showing queries).

Step 4: Determine the visual

Someone will need to review your work and use your model as input for future deliverables such as software development, so deciding on the most useful visual is an important step. After getting an answer to Strategic Question #4, *Who is our audience?*, we know that Mary will be our validator.

There are many different ways of displaying the BTM. Factors include the technical competence of the audience and the existing tools environment.

However, it would be helpful to know which data modeling notations and data modeling tools are currently being used within the organization. If the audience is familiar with a particular data modeling notation—such as Information Engineering (IE), which we have been using throughout this book—that is the notation we should use. If the audience is familiar with a particular data modeling tool, such as IDERA's ER/Studio, erwin DM, or Hackolade Studio, and that data modeling tool uses a different notation, we should use that tool with that notation to create the BTM.

Luckily, the two BTMs we created, one for rules and one for queries, are very intuitive, so there is a very good chance our models will be well-understood by the audience.

Step 5: Review and confirm

Previously, we identified the person or group responsible for validating the model. Now, we need to show them the model and make sure it is correct. Often at this stage, after reviewing the model, we make some changes and then show them the model again. This iterative cycle continues until the validator approves the model.

Three tips

1. **Organization**. The steps you went through in building this "model" are the same steps we go through in building any model. It is all about organizing information. Data modelers are fantastic organizers. We take the chaotic real world and show it in a precise form, creating powerful communication tools.

2. **80/20 Rule.** Don't go for perfection. Too many requirements meetings end with unfulfilled goals by spending too much time discussing a minute particular issue. After a few minutes of discussion, if you feel the issue's discussion may take up too much time and not lead to a resolution, document the issue and keep going. You will find that for modeling to work well with Agile and other iterative approaches, you may have to forego perfection and sometimes even completion. Much better to document the unanswered questions and issues and keep going. Much better to deliver something imperfect yet still very valuable than to deliver nothing. You will find that you can get the data model about 80% complete in 20% of the time. One of your deliverables will be a document containing unanswered questions and unresolved issues. Once all of these issues and questions are resolved, which will take about 80% of your time to complete, the model will be 100% complete.

3. **Diplomat.** As William Kent said in **Data and Reality** (1978), *so, once again, if we are going to have a database about books, before we can know what one representative stands for, we had better have a consensus among all users as to what "one book" is.* Invest time trying to get consensus on terms before building a solution. Imagine someone querying on pets without having a clear definition of what a pet is.

Three takeaways

1. Six strategic questions must be asked before you begin any project (Step 1). These questions are a prerequisite to the success of any initiative because they ensure we choose the right terms for our BTM. Next, identify all terms within the scope of the initiative (Step 2). Make sure each term is clearly and completely defined. Then determine how these terms are related (Step 3). Often, you will need to go back to Step 2 at this point, because in capturing relationships, you may come up with new terms. Next, determine the most beneficial visual for your audience (Step 4). Consider the visual that would resonate best with those needing to review and use your BTM. As a final step, seek approval of your BTM (Step 5). Often at this point, there are additional changes to the model, and we cycle through these steps until the model is accepted.

2. Create a relational BTM in addition to a query BTM if you feel there would be value in capturing and explaining the participation and existence rules.

3. Never underestimate the value of precise and complete definitions.

CHAPTER 2

Refine

This chapter will explain the data modeling refine phase. We explain the purpose of refine, refine the model for our animal shelter case study, and then walk through the refine approach. We end the chapter with three tips and three takeaways.

Purpose

The purpose of the refinement stage is to create the logical data model (LDM) based on our common business vocabulary defined during the align stage. Refine is how the modeler captures the business requirements without complicating the model with implementation concerns, such as software and hardware.

The shelter's Logical Data Model (LDM) uses the common business language from the BTM to precisely define the business requirements. The LDM is fully-attributed yet independent of technology. We build the relational LDM by normalizing, covered in Chapter 1. Figure 55 contains the shelter's relational LDM.

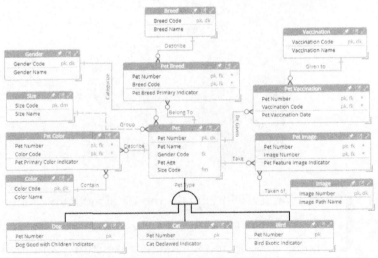

Figure 55: Animal shelter relational LDM.

This model does not change based on requirements. Therefore, we can use it as the starting point model for all queries. Let's briefly walk through the model. The shelter identifies each **Pet** with a **Pet Number**, which is a unique counter assigned to the **Pet** the day the **Pet** arrives. Also entered at this time are the pet's name (**Pet Name**) and age (**Pet Age**). If the **Pet** does not have a name, it is given one by the shelter employee entering the pet's information. The shelter employee entering the pet's information estimates the pet's age if unknown. If the **Pet** is a **Dog**, the shelter employee entering the information performs a few assessments to determine whether the Dog is good with children (**Dog Good With Children Indicator**). If the **Pet** is a **Cat**, the shelter employee determines whether the **Cat** has been declawed (**Cat Declawed Indicator**). If the Pet is a **Bird**, the shelter employee enters whether it is an exotic bird such as a parrot (**Bird Exotic Indicator**).

Approach

The refine stage is all about determining the business requirements for the initiative. The end goal is a logical data model which captures the attributes and relationships needed to answer the queries. The steps to complete appear in Figure 56.

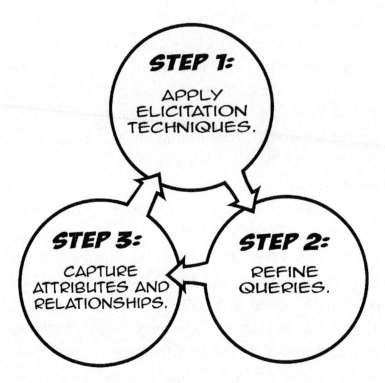

Figure 56: Refinement steps.

Similar to determining the more detailed structures in a traditional logical data model, we determine the more detailed structures needed to deliver the queries during the refinement stage. You can therefore call the query LDM a query refinement model if you prefer. The query refinement model is all about discovery and captures the answers to the queries that reveal insights into a business process.

Step 1: Apply elicitation techniques

This is where we interact with the business stakeholders to identify the attributes and relationships needed to answer the queries. We keep refining, usually until we run out of time. Techniques we can use include interviewing, artifact analysis (studying existing or proposed business or technical documents), job shadowing (watching someone work), and prototyping. You can use any combination of these techniques to obtain the attributes and relationships to answer the queries. Often these techniques are used within an Agile framework. You choose which techniques to use based on your starting point and the needs of the stakeholders. For example, if a stakeholder says, "I don't know what I want, but I'll know when I see it," building a prototype might be the best approach.

Analyze workloads

Every application has one or multiple workloads. It can be quite simple for a small application that just needs a handful of database operations or very complex for an ERP system with thousands of different queries and large degrees of customizations. What all applications have in common is that if they are successful, then new workloads and unforeseen use cases will arise. Imagine a shop application that starts simple (a typical OLTP use case) and soon needs support for analytical queries to measure the success of an ads campaign. Choosing a future-proof database product is therefore a good investment!

Before JSON-relational duality, a user would have to choose between a relational database and a (JSON) document database. Relational databases are very mature and easily support different workloads and future queries (we call that *use-case flexible*). At the same time, relational databases are often perceived as much harder to work with for agile application development because they fully expose the storage model (the tables and columns) to the application developer. This complicates easy database operations because application objects are decomposed into multiple tables and require joins to reassemble them.

Because of these characteristics of relational databases, many developers started to use NoSQL databases, especially so-called *document databases*. These store application objects as (JSON) objects and do not require mapping and decomposing them to multiple tables, allowing for retrieving objects without complex queries and joins. In addition, because JSON has no schema, it was easy to evolve the application by just adding new fields to the JSON data. We call this *'schema-flexible'*.

However, choosing a document database often means sacrificing use-case flexibility because the JSON structure can only handle one way to access data. We need to duplicate the same data across multiple JSON documents to support multiple use cases, which can cause data inconsistencies.

Luckily, Oracle's new paradigm, JSON-relational duality, obsoletes this choice as users can use both a relational model and a JSON document model simultaneously. They get the use-case flexibility of the relational model together with the easy access that JSON provides.

But this does not mean that the user does not have to think about workloads! It is still important to understand to what extent data normalization is required or beneficial for the workloads. For example, Oracle database supports JSON as a column data type, making it possible to store JSON substructures in a JSON column instead of normalizing them to the same or another table.

The good news is that both reads and writes are supported on both the relational tables as well as one or multiple duality views. This makes it possible to find the best access pattern for each workload without replicating data or worrying about inconsistencies.

A little side note: Oracle database, as a very mature enterprise-class database, offers many features you can use with duality views, such as fast refreshable materialized views to 'precompute' complex queries, various indexing, spatial processing, caches, and so one. This book does not go into the details of workloads using duality views that can be further tuned or optimized.

You may use a spreadsheet or any other method to document the results of your workload analysis based on the example in Figure 57, which is built into Hackolade Studio for Oracle duality views.

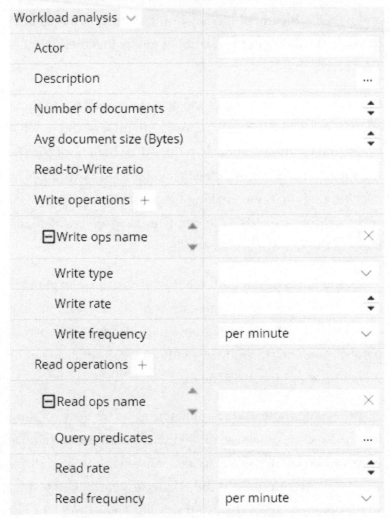

Figure 57: Workload analysis data capture screen.

When considering schema evolution later in the lifecycle, you will be able to review the values originally recorded, as reality might be very different than what was originally estimated. You should document the query predicates with the specific expression and parameters used to determine which documents should be retrieved.

Quantify relationships

Since entity-relationship diagrams were first introduced, we have relied on zero, one, and many to represent the cardinalities of relationships. This method has been generally suitable for a long time, but the world has evolved. Today's datasets are significantly larger than before. Failing to recognize that the "many" in a relationship can sometimes mean thousands or even millions of objects, can create new challenges when embedding, retrieving, or joining these objects in applications.

As these vast relationships have become more common, it is advisable to quantify them more precisely, instead of the ambiguous term "many." For instance, rather than using [0, M] to denote that an object can be linked to zero-to-many other objects, we should specify the order of magnitude. For example, a product might have [0, 1000] reviews, which is more informative and helps us think about pagination or other ways to limit the number of reviews per product.

To further clarify the relationships, we can include an optional "most likely" or "median" value. For example, [0, 20, 1000] provides even more details by indicating that a product may have between 0 and 1000 reviews, with a median of 20. When using Hackolade Studio to create our model, we can represent arrays in a document with the cardinalities shown in Figure 58.

Quantification ⌄		
Minimum	0	⏶⏷
Min unit	single	⌄
Likely	20	⏶⏷
Likely unit	single	⌄
Maximum	1000	⏶⏷
Max unit	single	⌄

Figure 58: Cardinalities.

We will inevitably make errors in estimating these numbers initially, but we should aim to get the order of magnitude correct. If not, it signals a need to review the model, as it may indicate that some information should be referenced instead of embedded.

A crucial factor for JSON array values is whether they are referenced by other documents or collections. If there are no other references and the array is relatively small, it might be sensible to store it in a JSON-type column within the same table as the non-array value. This approach avoids the need to join with another table that would typically result from normalization. For instance, the available colors of a product are few and always needed when loading the product, making them suitable for storage in the same table.

However, if an array can become very large, such as all the reviews for a product, it is more practical to store them separately, especially if not all reviews are loaded when retrieving the product. If the content of an array is shared with other documents (within the same or another collection), it should be stored in a separate table, similar to a conventional relational data model.

Step 2: Refine queries

The refinement process is iterative, and we keep refining, again, usually until we run out of time.

Step 3: Capture attributes and relationships

Ideally, because of the hierarchical nature of document (and also key-value) databases, we should strive to answer one or more queries with a single structure. Although this might seem "anti-normalization", one structure organized to a particular query is much faster and simpler than connecting multiple structures. The logical data model contains the attributes and related structures needed for each of the queries identified in the query refinement model.

Using artifact analysis, we can start with the animal shelter's logical and use this model as a good way to capture the attributes and relationships within our scope. Based on the queries, we do not need quite a few of our concepts for searching or filtering, and so they can become additional descriptive attributes on the **Pet** entity.

For example, no critical queries involved vaccinations. Therefore, we can simplify this model subset from the model in Figure 59 to the model in Figure 60.

Figure 59: Normalized model subset.

Figure 60: Denormalized model subset.

This example illustrates how traditional RDBMS models differ from NoSQL or Oracle duality views. In our original logical model, it was important to communicate that a **Pet** can receive many **Vaccinations** and a **Vaccination** can be given to many **Pets**.

In NoSQL, however, since there were no queries needing to filter or search by vaccination, the vaccination attributes just become other descriptive attributes of **Pet**. The **Vaccination Code** and **Vaccination Name** attributes are now a nested array within **Pet**. So, for example, if Spot the Dog had five vaccinations, they would all be listed within Spot's record (or *document* to use Oracle duality views terminology). Following this same logic, the pet's colors and images also become nested arrays, as shown in Figure 61.

In addition, to help with querying, we need to create a **Pet Type** structure instead of the Dog, Cat, and Bird subtypes. After determining the available pets for adoption, we need to distinguish whether the **Pet** is a **Dog**, **Cat**, or **Bird**. Our model would now look like what appears in Figure 62.

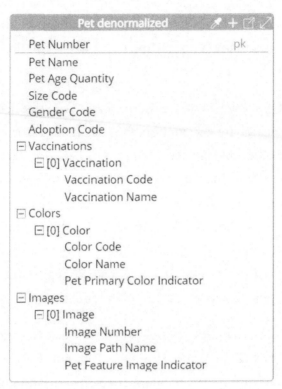

Figure 61: Nested arrays added for color and images.

In addition to the denormalization seen before, this example illustrates the polymorphic nature of Oracle duality views' document model as an alternative to the inheritance tables of relational databases. This single schema describes and can validate different document types for dogs, cats, and birds in addition to the common structure. Relational subtyping is accomplished here with the oneOf choice, which allows multiple subschemas.

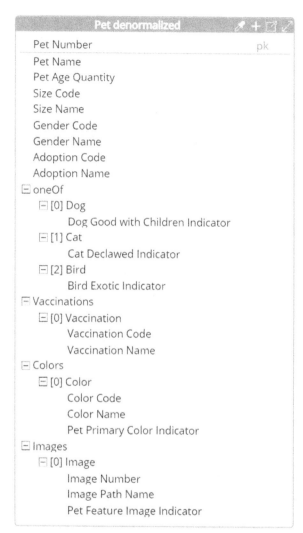

Figure 62: Our complete LDM with Pet Type.

Junction tables found in relational models are replaced here by arrays of subobjects, the array data type allowing for an ordered list of items.

Three tips

1. **Access patterns:** the query-driven approach is critical to leverage the benefits of Oracle duality views when creating an LDM. Don't be tempted by old normalization habits unless the workload analysis reveals relationship cardinality that warrants normalization.

2. **Aggregates:** keep together what belongs together! A nested structure in a single document can ensure atomicity and consistency of inserts, updates, and queries without expensive joins. It is also beneficial for developers who are used to working with objects, and it is easier to understand for humans.

3. **It is easier to normalize a denormalized structure than the opposite:** a normalized LDM is not technology-agnostic if it includes supertypes/subtypes or junction tables. Or it is "technology-agnostic" only if your physical targets are exclusively relational and don't include NoSQL databases or Oracle duality views. A denormalized LDM, on the other hand, can be easily normalized for relational physical targets by a good data modeling tool, while providing denormalized structures based on the access patterns identified earlier.

Three takeaways

1. The purpose of the refinement stage is to create the logical data model (LDM) based on our common business vocabulary, which we define for our initiative during the align stage. Refine is how the modeler captures the business requirements without complicating the model with implementation concerns, such as software and hardware.

2. An LDM is typically fully-attributed yet independent of technology. But this strict definition is being challenged nowadays with the fact that technology targets can be so different in nature: relational databases, the different families of NoSQL, storage formats for data lakes, pub/sub pipelines, APIs, etc.

3. It used to be, with relational databases, that you wanted to design a structure that could handle any possible future query that might be run down the road. With Oracle duality views, you want to design schemas that are specific, not only for an application, but for each access pattern (write or read) in that application. We should design the underlying relational schema to support all known and future access patterns. If an entity is shared (referred to), it should not be stored as a JSON value column of another entity.

CHAPTER 3

Design

This chapter will explain the data modeling design phase. We explain the purpose of design, design the model for our animal shelter case study, and then walk through the design approach. We end the chapter with three tips and three takeaways.

Purpose

The purpose of the design stage is to create the Physical Data Model (PDM) based on the business requirements defined in our logical data model. Design is how the modeler captures the technical requirements without compromising the business requirements, yet accommodating the initiative's software and technology needs used for the initiative.

The design stage is also where we accommodate history. We modify our structures to capture how data changes over time. For example, the Design stage would allow us to keep track of not just the most recent name for a pet, but also the original. For example, the animal shelter changes a pet's name from Sparky to Daisy. Our design could store the original pet name and the most current, so we would know Daisy's original name was Sparky. Although this is not a book on temporal data or modeling approaches that gracefully allow for storing high data volatility or varying history requirements, such as the Data Vault,[7] you would need to consider such factors in the Design stage.

Figure 63 below shows the Physical Data Model (PDM) of the animal shelter for a relational database (example uses

---

[7] For more on the data vault, read John Giles' *The Elephant in the Fridge*.

Microsoft Access). The design of the tables underlying one or multiple Oracle duality views looks very similar (the data type names would differ).

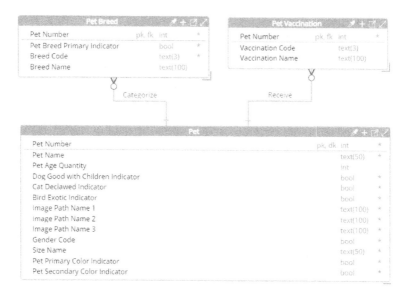

Figure 63: PDM of the shelter's Access database.

Note that the PDM includes formatting and nullability. Also, this model is heavily denormalized. For example:

- Although the logical communicates that a **Pet** can have any number of images, their design only allows up to three images for each **Pet**. The shelter uses **Image_Path_Name_1** for the featured image.

- Notice how we address the decode entities from the logical. We denormalize the one-to-many relationships into **Pet**. **Gender_Name** is not needed because everyone knows the codes. People are not familiar with **Size_Code,** so we only store **Size_Name**. We denormalize **Breed** into **Pet_Breed**. It is common to model decode entities in different ways on the physical, depending on the requirements.

- We denormalized **Vaccination** into **Pet_Vaccination**.

For Oracle duality views, it would look more like the model in Figure 64.

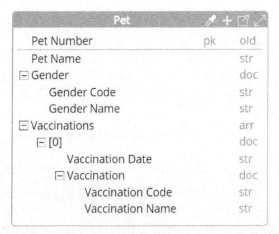

Figure 64: If modeling the shelter's database with Oracle duality views.

Approach

The design stage is all about developing the database-specific design for the initiative. The end goal is the query

PDM, which we can also call the *query design model*. For our animal shelter initiative, this model captures the Oracle duality views design and JSON interchange format for the initiative. The steps to complete appear in Figure 65.

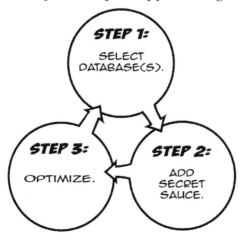

Figure 65: Design steps.

Step 1: Select database(s)

We now know enough to decide which database would be ideal for the application. Sometimes, we might choose more than one database if we feel it would be the best architecture for the application, although this often means replicating data and keeping it consistent. Architectures involving multiple databases add complexity (more moving parts) and increase maintenance costs (more experts needed), so most developers try to avoid them and stick to one, more powerful database. If you're not convinced yet, try to do a consistent point-in-time recovery with two databases.

We know in the consortium's case that they are using JSON for transport and Oracle duality views for storage. Oracle duality views allow SQL access to underlying tables and NoSQL. Access the JSON documents defined over the same tables so that data is kept consistent and can be shared across document collections. This enables us to run very different workloads (OLTP, analytical, reporting, etc.) on the same data with the same security model, transaction model, optimizer, etc.

Step 2: Secret sauce

The following lists capabilities of duality views that are not possible in pure JSON document databases. These capabilities are quite fundamental and can usually be combined to solve a specific use case as best as possible.

The presented capabilities capture the state of the Oracle 23ai database release 23.4. Future releases will have more as this whole space is under very active development.

The examples are for a simple sample application to manage a conference. Our conference consists of sessions, speakers, and attendees. Let's assume the application shows all sessions, allowing an attendee to pick sessions (create a schedule) and also show speakers of their sessions. A simple ER diagram with the three entities and their relationships appears in Figure 66.

Attendee
N
M
Session
N
1
Speaker

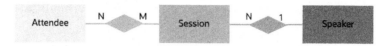

Figure 66: Conference application conceptual ER diagram.

First, we want to show that defining a single JSON hierarchy for our conference application is not possible. There are multiple ways to nest the three entities into hierarchies, and each hierarchy is probably optimal for a single case. However, none will be optimal for all anticipated use cases, even in our simple application.

The session organizer may prefer a hierarchy that lists all sessions with nested (embedded) speaker info and attendees. See Figure 67

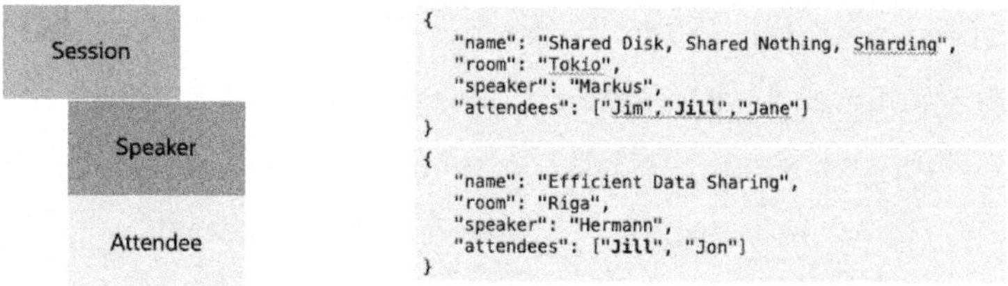

Session
Speaker
Attendee
{
"name": "Shared Disk, Shared Nothing, Sharding",
"room": "Tokio",
"speaker": "Markus",
"attendees": ["Jim","Jill","Jane"]
}
{
"name": "Efficient Data Sharing",
"room": "Riga",
"speaker": "Hermann",
"attendees": ["Jill", "Jon"]
}

Figure 67: Session hierarchy.

This hierarchy uses one document per **session**. It contains the speaker's name and serves well to populate a session catalog. But it also contains the attendees (which we would not want to show in the catalog), and even worse, attendees are being repeated. A specific attendee cannot simply find all their sessions as they must look into every session to see if their name is present in the nested array of names. An attendee would prefer to have one document with all their sessions. See Figure 68.

Figure 68: Attendee hierarchy.

Now, this hierarchy makes retrieving an attendee's schedule very easy as there is one JSON document for each **attendee** with all the information required for the use case of showing the attendee's schedule. But the speaker schedule, a slight modification of this use case, cannot be served with this JSON hierarchy: a speaker would have to look into each attendee's document to navigate to each session and see if they're the speaker to find out the room and time – extremely inconvenient! Instead, a third hierarchy is needed to manage the speaker schedule, with the speaker as the topmost entity.

We leave it to the reader to try out other hierarchies of the three entities. Hopefully, everyone will agree that different use cases require different data representations and, therefore, different JSON hierarchies!

In a pure JSON database, this poses a problem: JSON is not only the format for data exchange (data on the wire) but also the storage format (data on disk). Therefore, one or multiple compromises would have to be made, for example, storing the same data repeatedly and in different hierarchies. This leaves it to the application developer to keep the data consistent in different hierarchies. Data repetition makes this problem hard, as you may have many occurrences of the same information in different JSON documents. Imagine a session's time to be modified: you must check every attendee's document to see if they plan to attend.

An orthogonal but somewhat similar problem is the 'selection of values': Let's say a speaker has a phone number (we need to reach her in case she does not show up). We would not show this phone number in the session catalog or session schedule as this is private information. Nonetheless, a speaker's phone number is part of the speaker information, which we (partially) need in the above-mentioned use cases. Again, the application would have to prune private information from the JSON documents in a pure JSON database before sending it to a web browser. This also implies that the developer can see this data. This is a possible security leak, especially when private information like credit cards, health records, salaries, etc., needs to be managed.

JSON-relational duality to the rescue

Let's show how this can be elegantly solved with a normalized model and multiple duality views on top.

First, let's generate the tables. We start with the simplest form with a few columns to understand the concepts. Note that every table has a key (unique or primary), and relationships between tables can be declared using foreign keys. See Figure 69.

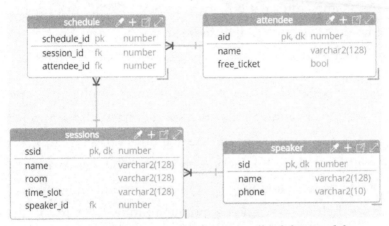

Figure 69: Conference application normalized data model.

The following SQL scripts show a minimum set of columns to capture an entity's data. It is possible to make these objects schema-flexible by adding a JSON type (flex) column. This is explained in the section with the title "Controlled schema flexibility." This means we can add new fields on the fly without defining them upfront as separate columns.

```
create table attendee(
  aid    number,
  name   varchar(128),
  free_ticket boolean,
  constraint attendee primary key (aid)
);
```

```
insert into attendee values(1, 'Steve', true);
insert into attendee values(2, 'Sophie', false);

create table speaker(
  sid     number,
  name    varchar(128),
  phone   varchar2(10),
  constraint pk_speaker primary key (sid)
);

insert into speaker values(1, 'Pascal', '123459');
insert into speaker values(2, 'Bodo', '555566');

create table sessions(
  ssid        number,
  name        varchar2(128),
  room        varchar2(128),
  time_slot   varchar2(128),
  speaker_id  number,
  constraint pk_session primary key (ssid),
  constraint fk_session
      foreign key (speaker_id)
      references speaker(sid)
);

insert into sessions values
  (1,'Intro to Hackolade','Room 1','10:00-10:45',1);

insert into sessions values
  (2, 'Data models 101', 'Room 2', '13:15-14:00',1);

insert into sessions values
  (3, 'Duality Views', 'Room 1', '9:00-9:45',2);
```

The most complex table is the 'schedule' table: it reflects the many-to-many relationship between attendee and session. It only consists of keys: a primary key for the session entry and two foreign keys to the 'attendee' and 'session' tables.

```
create table schedule (
  schedule_id number,
  session_id  number,
  attendee_id number,
  constraint pk_schedule primary key(schedule_id),
```

```
    constraint fk_schedule_attendee
        foreign key (attendee_id)
        references attendee(aid),
    constraint fk_schedule_session
        foreign key (session_id)
        references sessions(ssid)
);

insert into schedule values (1,1,1);
insert into schedule values (2,2,1);
insert into schedule values (3,2,2);
insert into schedule values (4,3,1);
```

An interesting aspect is that it only returns numbers if we query this 'schedule' table. So, for a human reader, gathering the actual information from the normalized table is pretty hard. Let's define duality views on top of these tables to see if that makes it simpler!

A duality view in its simplest form appears in Figure 70.

Figure 70: Speaker duality view entity.

It is a regular SQL query with a SQL/JSON generation function that generates a JSON object per row. The actual function name as per the standard is JSON_OBJECT(), but here we show the shorter equivalent syntax JSON{}. With Hackolade Studio, there is no need to know the syntax, as the script gets created automatically from the declaration of the view with a few clicks of the mouse.

```
create or replace JSON Duality view speakerDV as
select JSON {'_id' : sid,
             name,
             phone
            }
from speaker with insert update delete;
```

The clause 'with insert update delete' following the FROM clause specifies that we can update speaker information through this view as well as delete and insert new speakers. By default, a duality view is read-only. We will later see how this gives fine-grained control over the allowed changes.

This view, called 'speakerDV', exposes column values as fields inside a JSON document. Because the field names for 'name' and 'phone' are the same as the column names, we can simply list them in the object. Because we want the column 'sid' values to match a JSON key named '_id', we must use a syntax that separates the key's name and value with a colon.

Every duality view object must have a top-level field called '_id'. The corresponding value is unique per duality view.

Why do we need this '_id'? So that every tool knows how to identify an object, such as when caching it or accessing it over REST. This is why you will see an error if you try to declare a duality view without '_id'.

If we select from the speakerDV we will see the JSON objects that are being returned by the view.

```
select data from speakerDV;
{
  "_id" : 1,
  "name" : "Pascal",
  "phone" : "123459"
}

{
  "_id" : 2,
  "name" : "Bodo",
  "phone" : "555566"
}
```

The column name associated with the result is always called DATA. The view has no other columns. In that sense, a duality view is very similar to a JSON collection in NoSQL databases. Similarly, we create a duality view for the attendees. See Figure 71.

Figure 71: Attendee duality view entity.

```
create or replace JSON Duality view attendeeDV as
select JSON {
              '_id' : aid, name
            }
from attendee;
```

A lot more interesting is the duality view for an attendee's schedule as it required to join all four tables. As you will see, it is quite a long statement, accessing some columns of all participating tables. The statement also defines how to join them and assemble the values into a hierarchy of JSON objects and arrays. (Don't worry, there is a shorter syntax using GraphQL).

Figure 72: Schedule duality view entity.

```
create or replace JSON Duality view ScheduleDV AS
select JSON {
    '_id'      : a.aid,
    'name'     : a.name,
    'schedule' : [
        select JSON {
            'scheduleId' : sch.schedule_id,
            'session' : (
                select JSON {
                    ss.ssid,
                    ss.name,
                    ss.room,
                    'time' : ss.time_slot,
                    'speaker' : (
                        select JSON {
                            s.sid,
                            s.name
                        }
                        from SPEAKER s
                        where s.sid = ss.speaker_id)
```

```
              }
          from SESSIONS ss
          where ss.ssid = sch.session_id)
      }
    from SCHEDULE sch with insert delete
    where sch.attendee_id = a.aid
  ]
} from ATTENDEE a;
```

Some explanations:

- In the FROM clause, you see the table names (in uppercase here for better readability).

- The FROM clause can also be annotated with the allowed operations (with insert delete). In this duality view, we allow updates on the schedule object/table. A user can add or remove sessions, but they cannot update values inside a session, such as modify a speaker or change the room.

- The WHERE clause is used to join the tables. It uses joins on the primary key and foreign key columns. Our GraphQL version of the syntax does not need the user to declare those join conditions, it auto-derives them from the keys, saving the user some keystrokes.

- The SELECT list picks the columns of interest and maps them to fields in a JSON object. The field's values can map directly to a column or to the result of a subquery that generates either a JSON object or array. This defines the nesting.

- There is a bit of renaming happening here. Database column names often contain underscores when they're made of multiple words (like `session_id`). In JSON, underscores are uncommon. Instead, they're lowercase with the new word starting in uppercase (like `sessionId`). This is called camelCase. For names that need no renaming, the syntax is shorter: we just use the column name and the JSON field name is the same (like `room`).

Let's look at the output. Since we have two attendees, the view returns two schedules.

```
select data from ScheduleDV;
{
  "_id" : 1,
  "name" : "Steve",
  "schedule" :
  [
    {
      "scheduleId" : 1,
      "session" :
      {
        "ssid" : 1,
        "name" : "Intro to Hackolade",
        "room" : "Room 1",
        "time" : "10:00-10:45",
        "speaker" :
        {
          "sid" : 1,
          "name" : "Pascal"
        }
      }
    },
    {
```

```
          "scheduleId" : 2,
          "session" :
          {
              "ssid" : 2,
              "name" : "Data models 101",
              "room" : "Room 2",
              "time" : "13:15-14:00",
              "speaker" :
              {
                  "sid" : 1,
                  "name" : "Pascal"
                                            }
          }
      },
      {
        "scheduleId" : 4,
        "session" :
        {
            "ssid" : 3,
            "name" : "Duality Views",
            "room" : "Room 1",
            "time" : "9:00-9:45",
            "speaker" :
            {
                "sid" : 2,
                "name" : "Beda"
            }
        }
      }
  ]
}


{
  "_id" : 2,
  "name" : "Sophie",
  "schedule" :
  [
    {
      "scheduleId" : 3,
      "session" :
```

```
{
    "ssid" : 2,
    "name" : "Data models 101",
    "room" : "Room 2",
    "time" : "13:15-14:00",
    "speaker" :
    {
        "sid" : 1,
        "name" : "Pascal"
    }
}
    }
    ]
}
```

There are some aspects to mention:

- Every object contains the primary key. This information is needed when updating a duality view object: it allows us to identify the row that needs to change.

- By default, every table creates its own structure: a nested array or object. The use of an array makes sense for one-to-many relationships, as we expect more than one value to be returned. However, creating a sub-object for one-to-one relationships can be quite inconvenient when working with the application.

- Using the UNNEST keyword, we can 'merge' a nested object with its parent. For example, the speaker information can be merged into the session object.

Let's add two UNNEST keywords to merge the speaker and session object with the parent object. The UNNEST keyword comes in lieu of the field name associated with the merged sub-object. So choose field names to describe the value properly. Instead of `"speaker":{"id":1}`, we can choose something like `"speakerId ":1`. The following shows the updated statement to create a duality view with two unnested sub-objects:

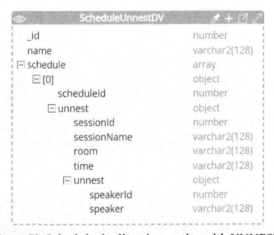

Figure 73: Schedule duality view entity with UNNEST.

```
create or replace JSON Duality view
ScheduleUnnestDV AS
select JSON {
   '_id'     : a.aid,
   'name'    : a.name,
   'schedule' : [
      select JSON {
          'scheduleId' : sch.schedule_id,
          UNNEST  (
              select JSON {
                  'sessionId' : ss.ssid,
                  'sessionName' : ss.name,
```

```
                ss.room,
                'time' : ss.time_slot,
                UNNEST  (
                    select JSON {
                        'speakerId': s.sid,
                        'speaker' : s.name
                    }
                    from speaker s
                    where s.sid = ss.speaker_id)
            }
            from sessions ss
            where ss.ssid = sch.session_id)
    }
    from schedule sch with update insert delete
    where sch.attendee_id = a.aid
  ]
} from attendee a;
```

The output of the view is now a bit simpler. We only show the second document for Sophie:

```
{
  "_id" : 2,
  "name" : "Sophie",
  "schedule" :
  [
    {
      "scheduleId" : 3,
      "sessionId" : 2,
      "sessionName" : "Data models 101",
      "room" : "Room 2",
      "time" : "13:15-14:00",
      "speakerId" : 1,
      "speaker" : "Pascal"
    }
  ]
}
```

As mentioned, there is a shorter syntax to define a duality view using GraphQL syntax. It is a bit shorter as it automatically knows how to join the participating tables based on primary and foreign key information.

```
create or replace JSON Duality view ScheduleDV AS
attendee
{
  _id: aid
  name        : name
  schedule    : schedule  @insert @delete
  {
    scheduleId : schedule_id
    sessions @unnest
    {
      sessionId : ssid
      name       : name
      room       : room
      time       : time_slot
      speaker @unnest
      {
          speakerId : sid
          speaker    : name
      }
    }
  }
} ;
```

Duality – data is both Tables and JSON documents at the same time

One of the most obvious benefits of this approach lies in the 'duality': it is possible to work with the same data using operations directly on the tables as well as on the JSON documents returned by the duality views. This gives great flexibility for application development and also allows developers to use their preferred access method:

- An application developer may choose to work only with JSON documents, such as using REST (see below) or a document store API.

- A data analyst likely prefers to use SQL (or a tool that generates SQL) over the same data. The access pattern is different. Instead of working with individual documents like the application developer, the analyst likely looks at aggregated information across thousands or millions of documents.

- An enterprise architect can simply modernize an existing (legacy) relational application by adding duality views on top.

- SQL is the preferred method for bulk operations as one can quickly update a table that underlies one or multiple duality views.

Duality views are an attempt to build a bridge between two camps: the SQL and NoSQL schools of thought. Both have their right to exist, but ideally, they should be in one data management system with consistent data.

SQL + NoSQL APIs

Last but not least, duality views do not only support SQL as language, but they can also be easily Auto-REST enabled using a tool called ORDS: short for Oracle Rest Data Service.

Figure 74: Auto-REST.

Even better, the Oracle database API for MongoDB supports duality views. This means that you can access (read, write, ...) JSON duality views with MongoDB's tools like compass, mongoShell, mongoexport, and MongoDB drivers as if duality views were MongoDB collection. All of the great features still apply, like data sharing, optimistic locking, etc. Figure 75 shows MongoDB compass with an Oracle error message after the user tries to update a read-only field in a duality view object.

Figure 75: Oracle duality view in MongoDB Compass.

Figure 76 shows how we REST enable a duality view.

```
1    // 20240124234641
2    // https://oraclejson.com/ords/beda/speakerv/
3
4  ▾ {
5  ▾    "items": [
6  ▾       {
7             "_id": 1,
8             "name": "Beda",
9             "boothDuty": "NO",
10 ▾          "_metadata": {
11               "etag": "8D742CF16BC7F1408A5D6EFB5AEE2BFA",
12               "asof": "0000000001D8E3FF"
13             },
14 ▾          "links": [
15 ▾             {
16                  "rel": "self",
17                  "href": "https://oraclejson.com/ords/beda/speakerv/1"
18                }
19             ]
20          },
21 ▾       {
22             "_id": 2,
23             "name": "Pascal",
24             "boothDuty": "YES",
25 ▾          "_metadata": {
26               "etag": "944004716SFFA26E80D0570968D799A2",
27               "asof": "0000000001D8E3FF"
28             },
29 ▾          "links": [
30 ▾             {
31                  "rel": "self",
32                  "href": "https://oraclejson.com/ords/beda/speakerv/2"
33                }
34             ]
```

Figure 76: REST-enabled duality view.

Only select what's needed

JSON from JSON-relational duality views do not persist as is. Instead, it maps to normalized tables consisting of rows and columns. Because the JSON documents are 'virtual', it is possible to define as many access patterns as needed using different duality views. These views can be partially overlapping, such as if one view selects more or different columns than another view. Therefore, it is possible (and recommended) to only select the values needed in a particular use case. A good example is a speaker's phone number:

- In the schedule documents, this field is deliberately missing and the column is not selected.

- For a session organizer, this field may be visible but read-only.

- In a third view this field is updateable.

JSON-relational duality inherits the use-case flexibility of the relational model. I can have as many views as I need, and each view only needs to select what is truly needed.

Being able to cherry-pick what to include in a JSON object not only makes them fit the use case but also minimizes the amount and kind of data that leaves the database. This can be very useful for data privacy or even security information as the rules can be enforced centrally in the database and audited. There is no way that a rogue application developer who is given access to a duality view with limited content can see the non-selected data that is not part of the view definition.

Sharing values across documents and collections

If you look at Steve's schedule you see that he is attending my talk. The nested object looks something like this:

```
{
   "sessionName" : "Duality Views",
   "room" : "Room 1",
   "speaker" : "Bodo",
   . . .
}
```

But there is a problem: My name is 'Beda', not 'Bodo'.
Someone made a mistake when adding my name. Let's fix
this. In a NoSQL JSON database, we would have to visit
every schedule document that contains the wrong name to
correct it. With duality views, this is much easier. We only
have to change the name once because it is stored in one
column of the 'speaker' table. We could directly update the
underlying table or run an update on the 'speakerDV'
duality view (remember we declared it 'with update').

```
update speakerDV s
set s.data = '{
   "_id" : 2,
   "name" : "Beda",
   "phone" : "555566"
}'
where s.data."_id" = 2;
```

The idea behind this update is that the object gets modified
in the application and then sent back to the database. We
call that a 'full document' update or replacement. It's also
possible to perform piece-wise updates. Although there are
different APIs that an application could call for this
operation, let's focus on regular SQL updates, such as those
issued by a Java program using JDBC. Because this is a SQL

update, we must specify in the WHERE clause which document to update. We do this by providing the _id value.

Any duality view using the speaker table will now see the updated value. If we query `ScheduleDV` after the update, we see the change:

```
{
  "sessionName" : "Duality Views",
  "room" : "Room 1",
  "speaker" : "Beda",
  ...
}
```

This is probably the biggest benefit of duality views compared to NoSQL databases that store JSON documents: the contents of documents can be shared across collections. This simplifies updates and guarantees consistency. It also means you can create many different JSON hierarchies over the same data. You no longer have to pick one JSON hierarchy!

As most real-world models are networks (or graphs) of information, duality views drastically simplify exposing the information in multiple JSON hierarchies that can share the same data.

Intra-document update control

Back to our conference: the `ScheduleDV` was designed for attendees to manage their schedules. They can add or remove sessions to their schedule array.

```
update ScheduleDV s
set s.data = JSON_Transform(s.data,
    APPEND '$.schedule' = JSON('
  {
      "scheduleId" : 4,
      "sessionId" : 3,
      "sessionName" : "Duality Views",
      "room" : "Room 1",
      "time" : "9:00-9:45",
      "speakerId" : 2,
      "speaker" : "Beda"
    }
'))
where s.data."_id" = 2;

1 row updated.
```

This is a piece-wise update where Sophie appends the talk 'Duality Views' to her schedule. As expected, this update succeeds as we allowed the array of sessions to be updated. Similarly, we can remove the session we just added:

```
update ScheduleDV s
set s.data = JSON_Transform(s.data,
                remove '$.schedule[1]')
where s.data."_id" = 2;
```

Now what would happen if Sophie tried to change the room of Pascal's session? You get an error!

```
update ScheduleDV s
set s.data = JSON_Transform(s.data,
        SET '$.schedule[0].room' = 'Parking Lot')
where s.data."_id" = 2;

ERROR at line 1:
ORA-40940: Cannot update field 'room' corresponding to
column 'ROOM' of table 'SESSIONS' in JSON Relational
Duality View 'SCHEDULEDV': Missing UPDATE annotation or
NOUPDATE annotation specified.
```

In this duality view, we can add or remove objects to the array of session, but no other changes are allowed. If we wanted to allow updating data about speakers or session, we could add corresponding annotations. But that is probably not the right solution here as this particular duality view serves one purpose (or workload): allowing attendees to manage their schedules. It would be better to just create another duality view to manage the session information (and don't give attendees access to that view).

Duality views allow you to centrally define what parts of an object can be modified and whether subobjects can be added or deleted. Defining this centrally in the database ensures that every application or client follows the rules. If you had to solve this outside the database, then the same rules have to be added and enforced in each application.

Controlled schema flexibility

Schema flexibility is a core characteristic of JSON. Unlike XML data, which almost always has a DTD or XML Schema defining what an XML instance meant, JSON started as a data format without the need for a schema: data types can be distinguished by the syntax of the values (the number 3 is not the string "3") and the array of one item ([3]) is not the item itself. All this information can be derived from a JSON instance document.

That said, the lack of a central schema does not mean that there is no schema at all. More likely, the schema is implicit in the application code. Every reader and writer assumes that the JSON data follows a certain shape and if this assumption is not honored, then the application may not function as intended.

Therefore, having the ability to define a central schema has some merits. By mapping JSON to normalized tables with columns, there is already a strong schema enforcement. If a JSON document cannot be mapped to the underlying tables of a duality view, an insert or update operation must fail. This strict schema may be desired for some applications, but it leaves a key benefit of JSON out: the ability to add new fields when the application evolves.

JSON-relational duality views can be 'opened' for schema flexibility by using a so-called 'flex column': this is a JSON-type column that stores all fields that cannot be mapped to relational columns of a table.

Figure 77 and Figure 78 show a schema flexible duality view for speakers.

speaker_flex		
sid	pk	number
name		varchar2(128)
phone		varchar2(10)
flex		json

Figure 77: Speaker table with flex column.

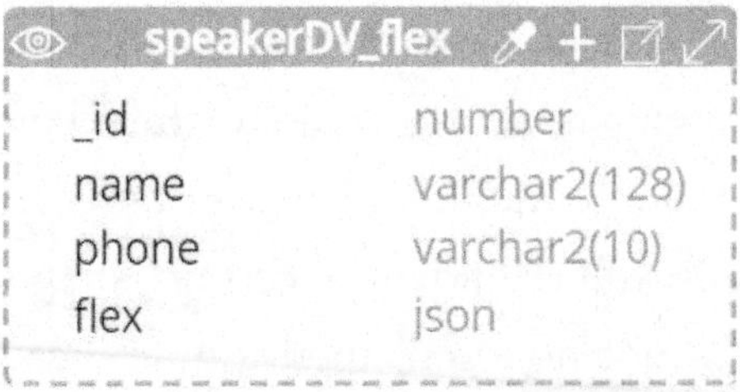

Figure 78: Speaker duality view with flex column.

The differences to the original example are highlighted in bold italic. As you can see, there is no column for the field 'company', but the insert still succeeded. The field and its value were added to the column 'flex', and during the SELECT, the content was merged with the parent object.

Now, schema flexibility is a two-edged sword: it is great if used wisely but can also lead to chaos, which is why proper data modeling is so important!

Please note that it is also possible to use JSON Schema to control the content of the flex column (see next secret sauce).

```
create table speaker(
  sid     number,
  name    varchar(128),
  phone   varchar2(10),
  flex    JSON (object),
  constraint pk_speaker primary key (sid)
);

create or replace JSON Duality view speakerDV as
select JSON {'_id' : sid,
             name,
             phone,
             flex as FLEX COLUMN
```

```
            }
from speaker with insert update delete;

insert into speakerDV values ('
{
  "_id"     : 12,
  "name"    : "Pascal",
  "phone"   : "123459",
  "company" : "Hackolade"
}
');

select data from speakerDV;

{
  "_id" : 12,
  "name" : "Pascal",
  "phone" : "123459",
  "company" : "Hackolade"
}
```

JSON Schema

Oracle database supports JSON Schema for two purposes:

- **To validate:** We can associate a JSON schema with any JSON type columns (including the flex columns) to precisely define what fields are mandatory or optional and what the content should look like.

- **To describe:** Any database object, including a duality view, can be described as a JSON schema document which describes the JSON data, together with rules and attributes.

The following shows (a fragment of) the JSON schema for the attendee session object. It is generated by the database from the properties of duality views. With this schema, data can be validated on the client, but the information can also be used for tools and code generators.

```
select dbms_json_schema.describe('SCHEDULEDV');

{
  "title" : "SCHEDULEDV",
  "dbObject" : "SYS.SCHEDULEDV",
  "dbObjectType" : "dualityView",
  "dbObjectProperties" :["update", "check"],
  "type" : "object",
  "properties" :
  {
    "_id" :
    {
     "type" : "number",
     "dbFieldProperties" : ["check"]
    },
    "name" :
    {
      "type" :  ["string", "null"],
      "maxLength" : 128,
      "dbFieldProperties" : ["check"]
    },
    "schedule" :
    {
      "type" : "array",
      "items" :
        {
            "type" : "object",
            "properties" :
              {
                  "scheduleId" :
                    {
                        "type" : "number",
```

```
                    /// more here

                    "additionalProperties" : false

} } } } } }
```

Since Hackolade Studio is also a JSON Schema editor, you can easily design and maintain structures without knowing the intricacies of the JSON Schema syntax. Figure 79 shows the model representation of the above JSON Schema:

Figure 79: Oracle JSON schema of ScheduleDV.

Generated fields

Quite often, an application is interested in a value that can be derived from the actual data. For example, for an order document, we want the number of line items, which is the count of the items, in an embedded array. Similarly, we'd like to know the compensation (bonus + salary) for an employee who received a salary and a bonus.

Of course, the application could perform these calculations after retrieving the document, but this is error-prone, and every application that accesses the same data will have to reimplement these same rules again.

Wouldn't it be easier if the view could directly generate these derived values?

JSON-relational duality views support generated fields in two flavors:

- **SQL expression:** these are expressions on the underlying column of a table. For example, a new field 'totalComp' can be defined as follows: 'totalcomp': generated using (SALARY + BONUS)

- **JSON path expression:** sometimes the values for the calculation are not readily accessible as columns of the underlying tables. Instead, the calculation may depend on values in the generated JSON output. We can access theses value easily when using JSON path expressions. The following example shows how we add a new field 'numSessions' to an attendee's schedule:

```
create or replace JSON Duality view ScheduleDV AS
select JSON {

  '_id'           : a.aid,
  'name'          : a.name,
  'schedule' : [
    select JSON {
        'scheduleId' : sch.schedule_id,
        'session' : (
            select JSON {
                ss.ssid,
                ss.name,
                ss.room,
                'time' : ss.time_slot,
```

```
                'speaker' : (
                    select JSON {
                        s.sid,
                        s.name
                    }
                    from SPEAKER s
                    where s.sid = ss.speaker_id)
                }
            from SESSIONS ss
            where ss.ssid = sch.session_id)
       }
    from SCHEDULE sch with insert delete
    where sch.attendee_id = a.aid
  ] ,
  'numSessions' : generated using path
  '$.schedule.size()',
  'initials' : generated using substr(name, 1,2)
} from ATTENDEE a;
```

The resulting schema for the duality view appears in Figure 80.

Figure 80: Schedule duality view entity with generated fields.

The path expression '$.schedule.size()' navigates to the 'schedule' array and counts the number of items. The second generated field, 'initial', just selects the first two characters from the name – substr is a SQL expression. The corresponding output shows new fields:

```
{
  "_id" : 1,
  "name" : "Steve",
  "schedule" :
  [
    {
      "scheduleId" : 1,
      "session" :
      {
        "ssid" : 1,
        "name" : "Intro to Hackolade",
        "room" : "Room 1",
        "time" : "10:00-10:45",
      }

/// more

  ],
  "numSessions" : 3,
  "initials" : "St"
}
```

We ignore generated fields on inserts or updates. They're truly derived values. The JSON schema that describes a duality view will mark these values as generated to distinguish them from persisted values.

```
"numSessions" :
    {
      "type" : ["number",          "null"],
      "dbFieldProperties" :["generated"]
    }
```

Another interesting use-case for generated fields is to mask or truncate the original values for views that are not supposed to see the entire values. A good example would be the 'last 4 digits of the social security number' for authentication or putting salaries into broader brackets using a case statement.

Generated fields also allow for checking system parameters. For example, we could check the language settings and pick a field's value in the language a user specified. Therefore, the same duality view can return JSON documents with different field values depending on the language, time zone, or other settings. For example, the following code shows how to fetch the right value from a language lookup table:

```
'conditionText' : generated using (
    select text        from productCondition pc
    where pc.condition_code = p.condition
    and pc.language_code = USERENV ('lang'))
```

Data partitioning

Imagine you have an entity like 'purchase order' where you want to treat orders differently. For example, depending on their order total amount or if this is the first order from a customer. In this case, we partition the totality or orders into different groups. This sounds complex but it's actually very easy as we just have to add a WHERE clause to the duality view definition. The following example shows a new duality view for all speakers with a US phone number (+1 country code).

```
create or replace JSON Duality view us_speakerDV as
select JSON {'_id' : sid,
             name,
             phone
             }
from speaker with insert update delete
where phone like '+1' with check option;
```

Figure 81: Speaker duality view entity with data partitioning.

You can create as many duality views as you want on the same underlying tables. The partitions can overlap.

Built-in optimistic concurrency control without locking

Every application that serves many users at the same time faces the same issues of concurrent updates and stale data:

- If I update a speaker, what if someone else has already done that and I would overwrite the data?

- What if the session catalog says Pascal's talk is at 10 o'clock where I have time to attend, but while I add it to my schedule, the time changes and I can no longer attend?

There are two common solutions, and neither is good:

1. The application could just lock a document to get exclusive access. For example, while I work on speaker X, no one else can update it. Although this may work fine for simple use cases, locking soon falls short:

    ◎ More complex applications may need to conditionally update more than one document. Locking all potential documents upfront may be impossible or reduce the amount of concurrency the system can handle. Lazy locking may cause very rare but hard-to-debug deadlocks.

    ◎ It may be acceptable for some (larger objects) if some values get changed, as not everything is equally important. For example, I may consider the room of a talk less important than the time. Adding a session to my schedule is ok if the room changes but a time change can cause a conflict.

    ◎ For stateless protocols like REST, locking is an immediate no-go. There is no guarantee that a document will ever be unlocked.

2. Another approach is to version the documents and only allow the update if the version has not changed. This requires applications to check for all updates to the version. A relational backend may not detect changes in substructures unless the versioning scheme is applied at every level (a

document full of version). Also, the version number does not really guarantee anything. Someone could send an update that does not change anything but still increments the version, thus invalidating updates from others and, if we have a cache, unnecessarily invalidating cache entries. And again, the versioning scheme treats all updates the same. Updating the room is the same as updating the time.

So, how do we solve that with duality views?

Simple: every document has an ETag value. ETag is a concept of http headers, giving each resource a version. For duality views, you can think of the ETag as a checksum of all participating values. If one or more values change, then the ETag checksum will have a different value. By default, all values of a duality view appear in the eTag calculation, but you can mark specific columns to be excluded. Therefore, an update that does not change a 'CHECK ETAG' column will not change the value of the checksum. Let's look at an example and create the following duality view for sessions:

Figure 82: Session duality view entity.

```
create or replace JSON Duality view sessionDV as
select JSON {'_id' : ssid,
                name,
                room WITH NOCHECK,
                'time' : time_slot
             }
from sessions with insert update delete;
```

The field/column 'room' has been annotated with 'NOCHECK'; this means that its value does not participate in the ETag checksum calculation.

But where is this ETag value in the document? This is something we have omitted so far in our examples! It is actually in every document inside a 'metadata' field:

```
select data from sessionDV;

{
  "_id" : 1,
  "_metadata" :
  {
    "etag" : "AABFD535CB52479A8A61F23076168C91",
    "asof" : "0000000001D8CBC9"
  },
  "name" : "Intro to Hackolade",
  "room" : "Room 1",
  "time" : "10:00-10:45"
}

{
  "_id" : 2,
  "_metadata" :
  {
    "etag" : "3240D59478CFC4121ECC0886747A68BD",
    "asof" : "0000000001D8CBC9"
  },
  "name" : "Data models 101",
```

```
  "room"  :  "Room 2",
  "time"  :  "13:15-14:00"
}


{
  "_id"  :  3,
  "_metadata"  :
  {
    "etag"  :  "447A5B736E026A8EDDE7E5039858C6FD",
    "asof"  :  "0000000001D8CBC9"
  },
  "name"  :  "Duality Views",
  "room"  :  "Room 1",
  "time"  :  "9:00-9:45"
}
```

When updating a document, the metadata object with the ETag field can either be omitted or returned. If it is omitted, the database does not check if the data is still current (still has the same ETag value). However, if the application includes the metadata with the ETag, the database will ensure that the ETag is still valid before completing the update. If the ETag no longer matches the update, it will abort with an error and the application can refetch the current data and attempt a second update.

Let's see how the ETag detects such conflict.

Step 1: Pascal (speaker) and Sophie (attendee) **both** fetch the same conference session.

```
select data
from sessionDV s
where s.data."_id" = 1;
```

```
{
  "_id" : 1,
  "_metadata" :
  {
    "etag" : "AABFD535CB52479A8A61F23076168C91",
    "asof" : "0000000001D8D1B7"
  },
  "name" : "Intro to Hackolade",
  "room" : "Room 1",
  "time" : "10:00-10:45"
}
```

Step 2: Pascal updates the time because his plane got delayed.

```
update sessionDV s
set s.data = JSON ('
  {
    "_id" : 1,
    "_metadata" :
    {
      "etag" : "AABFD535CB52479A8A61F23076168C91",
      "asof" : "0000000001D8D1B7"
    },
    "name" : "Intro to Hackolade",
    "room" : "Room 1",
    "time" : "16:00-16:45"
  }
')

1 row updated.
```

Step 3: After looking at the session catalog, Sophie decides to add Pascal's session to her schedule. She is not aware that the time has changed.

```
update sessionDV s
set s.data = JSON ('
  {
```

```
    "_id" : 1,
    "_metadata" :
    {
      "etag" : "AABFD535CB52479A8A61F23076168C91",
      "asof" : "0000000001D8D1B7"
    },
    "name" : "Intro to Hackolade",
    "room" : "Room 1",
    "time" : "16:00-16:45"
  }
')
where s.data."_id" = 1;

ORA-42699: Cannot update JSON Relational Duality View
'SESSIONDV': The ETAG of document with ID 'FB03C10200' in
the database did not match the ETAG passed in.
```

Sophie's update fails. She has to fetch the document again, make sure the time is still convenient, and then repeat the update.

If Pascal had only changed the room of his session, Sophie's update would have succeeded because the room field/column is excluded from the ETag calculation. What a simplification for the application developer to have optimistic locking built-in!

Polymorphism

Polymorphism means that 'things come in different shapes'. They may share some common attributes but differ in others. Let's look at an example. A person may have multiple accounts with their bank. Each account has an account number and a balance. Still, not every account is the same: a savings account has an interest rate, a checking account has an overdraft limit, and a brokerage account consists of the securities inside (the stocks or bonds).

Let's assume we want a JSON document that shows a customer with all their bank accounts. As you can see, the accounts are combined into a single array. Accounts have common attributes (name, balance, monthlyFee). But each account type has type-specific attributes. The brokerage account even has a nested array.

```json
{
    "id": 1,
    "person ": {
        "id": 1201,
        "name": "Jim"
    },
    "accounts": [
        {
            "accountId": 1,
            "name": "Standard Checking",
            "balance": 500,
            "monthlyFee": 5.99,
            "checkingId": 2,
            "overdraftLimit": 3.25
        },
        {
            "accountId": 2,
            "name": "Super Saver",
            "balance": 12000,
            "monthlyFee": 0,
            "savingsId": 2,
            "interestRate": 3.25
        },
        {
            "accountId": 3,
            "name": "Brokerage Pro",
```

```
        "balance": 55000,
        "monthlyFee": 0,
        "brokerageId": 3,
        "tradingLimit": 5000,
        "marginAllowed": false,
        "positions": [
            {
                "pid": 1,
                "quantity": 10,
                "symbol": "ORCL"
            },
            {

                "pid": 2,
                "quantity": 30,
                "symbol": "HCKLD"
            }
        ]
    }
  ]
}
```

We can represent the schema for the above JSON in Figure 83.

How can this be modeled with JSON Relational Duality? One obvious way would be to use a JSON-type (flex) column and just treat all custom data as flex data. Adding the polymorphism to the underlying relational schema is a better approach.

Savings, Checking, and Brokerage are subtypes. We create a separate table for each with their specific properties. Note that we need an additional table for the brokerage account to store the positions.

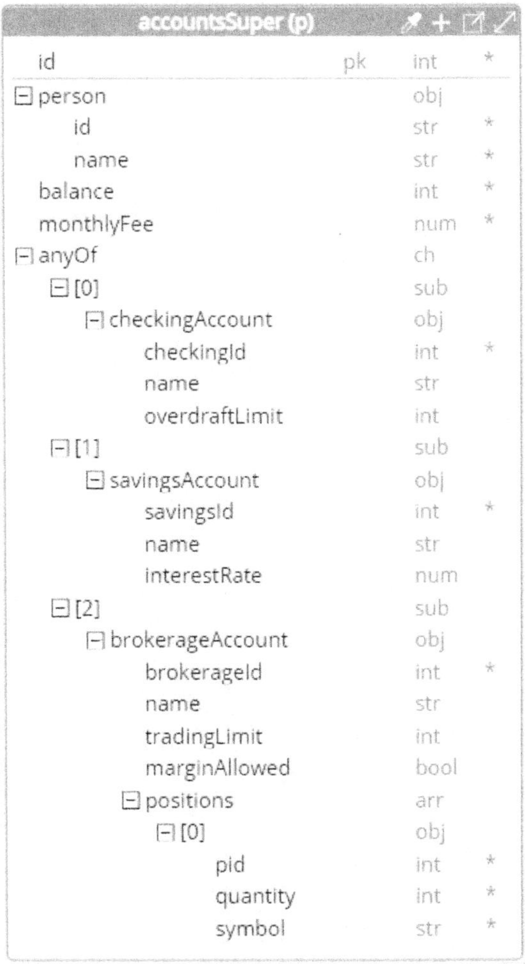

Figure 83: JSON Schema of polymorphic accounts.

```
create table checkingAccount(
    id              number primary key,
    overdraftLimit  number
);

create table savingsAccount(
    id          number primary key,
```

```
      interestRate number
);

create table brokerageAccount(
      id               number primary key,
      tradingLimit  number,
      marginAccount boolean
);

create table positions(
      id               number primary key,
      brokerageId number,
      quantity       number,
      symbol          varchar2(10),
      foreign key (brokerageId)
      references brokerageAccount(id)
);
```

Next, we create a table for the common attributes. This is the supertype for all account subtypes. In addition, it has pointers (foreign keys) to the corresponding subtype information.

```
create table accountsSuper (
      ID               number primary key,
      personId        number,
      balance         number,
      name            varchar2(20) not null,
      monthlyFee    number,
      brokerageID   number,
      savingsID       number,
      checkingID     number,
      foreign key (personID) references person(ID),
      foreign key (brokerageID)
                      references brokerageAccount(ID),
      foreign key (savingsID)
                      references savingsAccount(ID),
      foreign key (checkingID)
```

```
                        references checkingAccount(ID)
    );
```

Since this table refers to a person (each account belongs to a person), the following table needs to exist:

```
create table person
(
    id number primary key,
    name varchar2(20) not null
);
```

We can show the logical model for the above with a supertype and subtypes. See Figure 84.

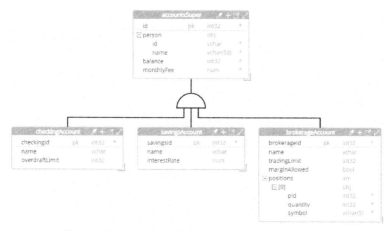

Figure 84: Logical model of polymorphic accounts.

Finally, we add the Duality view that ties all tables together. This view defines one document per person (customer) and contains an array that lists each account:

```
create JSON Duality View personWithAccountsV as
select JSON {
    '_id'       : p.ID,
```

```
'name'      : p.name,
'accounts' :
[
    select JSON
    {
        'accountId' : s.ID,
        'name'         : s.name,
        'balance'      : s.balance,
        'monthlyFee'   : s.monthlyFee,
        unnest (
            select JSON {
        'checkingId' : id,
        'overdraftLimit' :
                    checking.overdraftLimit}
            from checkingAccount checking
            where s.checkingID = checking.ID),
        unnest (
            select  JSON {
        'savingsId' : id,
        'interestRate' : savings.interestRate}
            from savingsAccount savings

            where s.savingsID = savings.ID),
        unnest (select  JSON {
        'brokerageId' : id,
        'tradingLimit' :
                    brokerage.tradingLimit,
        'marginAllowed' :
                    brokerage.marginAccount,
        'positions' :
        [
            select JSON
            {
                'pid':p.id,
                'quantity':p.quantity,
                'symbol':p.symbol
            }
            from positions p
            where p.brokerageId = brokerage.ID
        ]
        }
```

```
            from brokerageAccount brokerage
            where s.brokerageID =
            brokerage.ID)
         }
      from accountsSuper s
      where s.personId = p.id
   ]
}
from person p;
```

The view uses the unnest keyword to merge the attributes from the subtype object with the parent object. Therefore, the common attributes (supertype) and the specific attributes (subtype) appear in the same object. Figure 85 shows the corresponding Duality View model.

Figure 85: Duality View model of polymorphic accounts.

In the full model in Figure 86, we combine the relational tables and the Duality View.

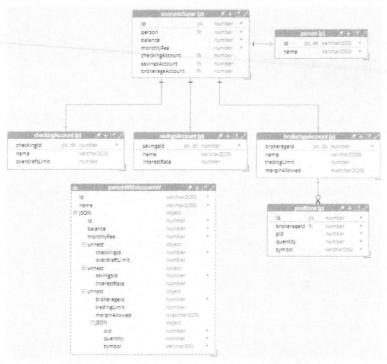

Figure 86: Combining the relational tables and the Duality View.

The example here uses classic data modeling for a relational application. Other approaches are feasible and can also be applied with JSON-relational duality.

Replace the ORM

Some readers may have already considered this: JSON-relational duality views are conceptually very similar to ORMs—Object Relational Mappers. Hibernate is a popular

ORM for the Java programming language. This brings us to the first advantage of JSON-relational duality: it is language independent. Centrally defined in one place, it allows any client to access the same object in the same manner. In addition, the generation of objects and the updates to all involved tables happen in the database, which reduces the number of database roundtrips to one. Not only do ORMs need multiple queries (roundtrips) to assemble more complex objects, but they also do not do that in a fully read-consistent manner, making it possible to read an inconsistent state. Optimist concurrency control is extremely hard to achieve for ORMs. Usually, version numbers have to be maintained in the database and in objects.

JSON-relational duality provides better performance, language independence, and higher data consistency than approaches outside the database kernel code.

Online application changes

JSON-relational duality views abstract data from multiple tables in one unit: the JSON document. An application expects the data to be in a consistent format/schema at a given time. For example, our sample conference application expects a session to have one speaker. This application may change over time. For example, we may realize that conference sessions may have multiple speakers. In that case, the application needs to be updated. This is relatively easy if there is only one version of the application running or if I can change and restart all application instances at the same time. For many applications, this is not possible, as older and newer versions of the application have to run simultaneously for a while until all clients get updated.

One approach used in JSON document stores is to add a version number to JSON documents, but this means that a newer document cannot be processed by an older application.

JSON Duality offers a new and better solution: When the data model changes (in our case, we evolve the application to allow for not just one but multiple speakers per session, likely by introducing a new NxM mapping table), we add a new duality view. We have one view that generates the new JSON where speaker is now a JSON array and a view for the old format, where we pick one speaker (or concatenate the speaker names). Because we can have arbitrarily many views over the same tables, we can give every client a view corresponding to the client's version.

Vectors and AI search

Oracle Database release 23ai provides a new SQL data type, VECTOR, and corresponding indexes for fast similarity search. We can create JSON-relational duality views on columns of type VECTOR and convert the vector information to a JSON representation, similar to an array. This way, it is possible to work with JSON documents containing one or multiple AI vectors. Similarity search becomes very easy and efficient if a vector index is created on that column.

A column of the type VECTOR is an array of embeddings, optionally defined with dimension and format parameters. The vector data type has different declaration formats that can be represented in the model and used to create the corresponding DDL.

Declaration format	Description
vector	Unknown number of dimensions and formats
vector(*.*)	Same as above
vector(nbr_of-dimensions,*)	Specify the number of dimensions without format
vector(nbr_of-dimensions)	Same as above
vector(*,element_format)	Unknown number of dimensions, but their format is specified (int8, float32, or float64)

For example, if our conference application had an abstract for each session, we could store a vector with the semantic information about each session in addition to the abstract text. The vector would be generated for the session abstract using AI embedding models. This could either happen in the database or outside the database.

The following example shows the DDL for the 'sessions' table with two additional columns: the abstract text and the vector for the semantic content.

```
create table sessions(
   ssid         number,
   name         varchar2(128),
   room         varchar2(128),
   time_slot    varchar2(128),
   abstract     varchar2(32767),
   content      vector,
   speaker_id   number,
   constraint pk_session primary key (ssid),
   constraint fk_session
       foreign key (speaker_id)
       references speaker(sid)
);
```

The model can display the number of dimensions and data type of embeddings. See Figure 87.

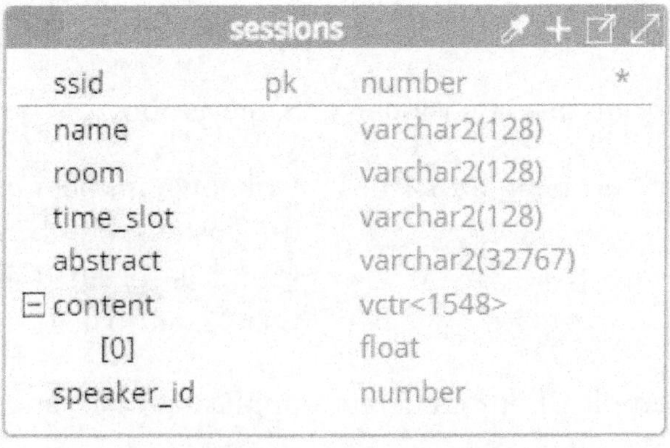

sessions			
ssid	pk	number	*
name		varchar2(128)	
room		varchar2(128)	
time_slot		varchar2(128)	
abstract		varchar2(32767)	
⊟ content		vctr<1548>	
[0]		float	
speaker_id		number	

Figure 87: Sessions data model with vector.

Time travel

You may have observed that there is another field in the metadata: 'asof'. What's that?

When a duality view assembles a JSON object from the underlying tables, rows, and columns, all values are from the exact point in time. Any concurrent writes won't affect the values in the JSON object. This is called read consistency. But what if your application issues separate queries? Then, each is at a different point in time and potentially not consistent. Let's say the application loads a conference schedule for one attendee in a first query and sometime later loads the speaker detail information from another duality view. If the speaker was deleted in the meantime, then this query would fail (which may be a good idea).

But would there be a way to read the speaker at the same point in time as the first query – basically traveling back in time? The answer is yes. The 'asof' property in the metadata of each duality view contains the point-in-time information to use in follow-up queries. Let's look at one example:

Step 1: Sophie queries her schedule:

```
{
  "_id" : 2,
  "_metadata" :
  {
    "etag" : "C5C6B8A0FFA14BEEA21617830E7F96FD",
    "asof" : "0000000000CA5DE9"
```

```
  },
  "name" : "Sophie",
  "schedule" :
  [
    {
      "scheduleId" : 3,
      "sessionId" : 2,
      "sessionName" : "Data models 101",
      "room" : "Room 2",
      "time" : "13:15-14:00",
      "speakerId" : 1,
      "speaker" : "Pascal"
    }
  ]
}
```

The field `"asof":"0000000000CA5DE9"` is the timestamp of this document. It can be used to query other duality views as of the same time. For example, to get read consistent results across different queries and views. It can also be used to view older values of the same document. The following example changes Sophie's name to Maria and commits the transaction. We can still see the older value when we use the asof value in the flashback query:

```
update attendee set name = 'Maria' where aid = 2;

commit;

select data from ScheduleDV
as of scn to_number('CA5E40','xxxxxx');

{
  "_id": 2,
  "name" : "Laura",
  "schedule" :
  ...
}
```

Automated data modeling

In general, developers and data architects prefer to design the schema for their applications. But this requires conceptual knowledge (we hope this book provides some of it!) as well as SQL skills to create tables, constraints, and, last but not least, the duality views on top of these tables. Oracle has a special treat for those (impatient) users who want to skip these steps and have the database suggest and create the relational backend. For this, a set of JSON documents (one or multiple collections) is analyzed by a tool called 'JSON to Duality Migrator'. In the first step, the structure and the values of the JSON documents are analyzed to identify keys, data types, and also values that are shared across documents. This information is then used to suggest a normalized set of tables (a schema) together with the duality views that generate the documents as they were presented to the tool. This recommendation is returned to the user as a JSON Schema document so that the user can inspect the proposed schema and modify it if needed. The tables and views are created in the second step, as defined in the JSON Schema document.

It is easy in the last step to reverse-engineer the instance with Hackolade Studio to generate the model with its Entity-Relationship Diagram, including duality views, for documentation and further evolution. See Figure 88.

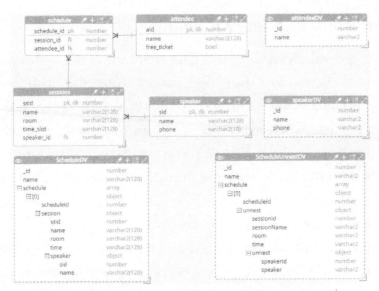

Figure 88: ER Diagram with tables and duality views.

JSON collection tables

JSON-relational duality is the modern data modeler's best friend. It combines strong normalization, like relational databases, with simple JSON representation, like document databases. In addition, schema flexibility can be controlled (or even disallowed).

But sometimes, even the most serious data modeler wants to be a cowboy and just store data without defining a schema. For example, when JSON data from a third-party source needs to be quickly queried.

For this, Oracle invented 'JSON collection tables'. These are pretty much regular tables, with one benefit: the user does not have to (and cannot) specify the 'shape' of the table. Instead, it always has just one column called "DATA". In addition, any JSON document that gets inserted into the collection must have a field called "_id". If such a field is absent, the database will assign a unique value. Consequently, working with a JSON collection is similar to working with one duality view. The shape is the same, and the same queries or DMLs can be executed, but no data sharing or partial update rules are supported. JSON collection tables have functionality similar to collections in JSON document databases. In fact, JSON collection tables, like duality views, are accessible via document store APIs like SODA or MongoDB tools using the 'Oracle Database API for MongoDB'.

The following shows the simple statement to create a collection table called 'speaker';

```
create JSON collection table speaker;
```

Next, we insert a simple document. Any syntactically correct JSON is supported here, as there is no schema assigned to this JSON collection table.

```
insert into speaker values ('
{
"speaker":"Beda",
"talks":[
    {
            "year": 2024,
            "type": "conference",
            "name": "Data Modeling Zone"
```

```
        },
        {
            "year": 2023,
            "type": "conference",
            "name": "Oracle Cloud World"
        },
        {
            "year": 2023,
            "type": "user group meeting",
            "name": "DOAG"
        },
        {
            "year": 2021,
            "type": "conference",
            "name": "IT-Tage"
        }
    ]
}');

1 row created.
```

The document itself has no identifying field. Instead, the database automatically assigns a _id field with a unique value.

```
select s.data."_id" from speaker s;

"6658111622fdfbaa9ebe2fe5"
```

While this kind of storage is extremely convenient, we all know that the value of data comes from being able to extract meaningful insights from it. So, to better understand schemaless documents stored in a JSON collection table, you may want to have a visual representation of the structure of the JSON document. To that effect, you may connect Hackolade Studio to reverse-engineer the table so its powerful algorithms can infer the schema from a sample of the documents in the table. See Figure 89.

The above document (as well as others in the sample) generated this table schema after inference:

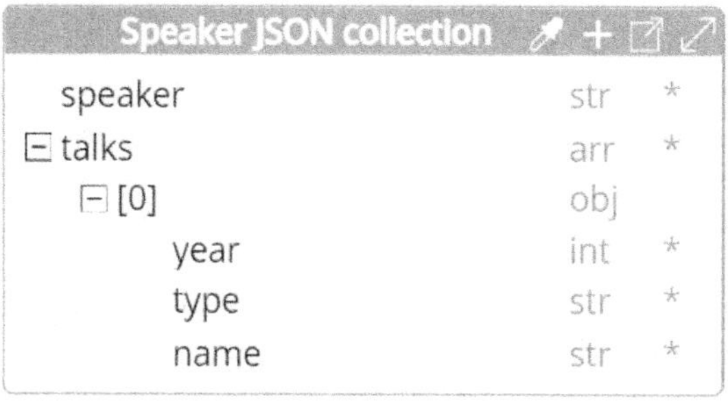

Figure 89: Inferred JSON collection schema.

We can now access this data using SQL, REST, or document APIs. As you can see in the above example, the data has a nested array of objects. Let's use a simple SQL operation to unnest the array into different rows:

```
select * from speaker NESTED data
   COLUMNS (speaker,
        NESTED '$.talks[*]' COLUMNS (name, year));

 SPEAKER      NAME
                                           YEAR
 ----------   ---------------------   ----------
 Beda         Data Modeling Zone      2024
 Beda         Oracle Cloud World      2023
 Beda         DOAG                    2023
 Beda         IT-Tage                 2021
```

This book does not explain Oracle's powerful and versatile operators to work with JSON. To learn more about this, please consult the official and free documentation 'JSON Developer Guide' and 'JSON-relational duality Developer's Guide'.

Three takeaways

1. **JSON-relational duality is a new paradigm for data modeling** that combines the use-case flexibility of the relational model with the use-case simplicity of JSON. Hierarchical data models (like JSON) are intuitive as real-world objects are projected into documents. But when storing documents, this simplicity comes at the expense of future use cases that need to view the same data in different shapes or only need to select some parts of the data – persisted JSON is not use-case flexible. This is where the relational model shines: because data is normalized and entities are stored separately, it is possible to access the data in any way, even the ones that are not known yet. With JSON-relational duality, one can define as many JSON 'access' views as needed. These views provide **use-case simplicity** while the underlying relational storage provides **use-case flexibility**. JSON-type columns provide **schema-flexibility**.

2. **JSON-relational duality enables proven data modeling techniques** and best practices for JSON-based development. Data modeling is a very important step when designing applications or data-driven systems. A wrong or incomplete data

model may lead to applications that are hard to extend or maintain, or that just perform badly. The good news is that data modeling is a well-established technique with many trained professionals that (among other things) guide development teams by translating business requirements into a commonly agreed data model that supports current and future requirements. Data modeling with duality views can, for the most part, be done exactly like it's done for relational applications. A new option is using JSON-type columns for nested objects (when denormalization would not be needed) or schema-flexibility to allow an application to add new fields on the fly. By adding JSON Relational Duality views, the data modeler gives access to the underlying data in a document format that is easy to work with for the given use cases. JSON Duality should be very easy to adopt by data modelers, architects, and developers who are used to the relational model.

3. **Include all stakeholders and domain experts early on.** JSON-relational duality is a very powerful feature with a broad set of capabilities. A developer (or development team) might be tempted to design an application by themselves. However, if the task has not been understood properly and an inferior data model has been designed, then reworking the underlying storage model might be required. A tool like Hackolade Studio makes it easy to analyze and record access patterns and application flows, as well as translate conversations with non-technical people into proper data models.

Conclusion

Oracle has introduced a truly novel approach for data modelers in database release 23ai. Data that is stored in normalized tables can be accessed as JSON documents for both read and write operations. Like an ORM, the JSON documents encapsulate information in one easy-to-work-with data unit, independent of how this data is stored on disk. Long-existing relational concepts, like normalized storage without data repetition, strong consistency, and fine-grained update rules, are finally becoming accessible to users who prefer working with JSON document databases. But the best part is really the 'duality': data is both relational and JSON at the same time, and users can work with the data however they prefer! It is no longer a choice to use relational or JSON. One can have both in one database.

JSON-relational duality is still under active development, with many features planned that this book does not cover. We advise regularly checking Oracle's public websites for updates to this feature.

As seen throughout the book, data modeling is critical to ensure communication, quality, consistency, and governance. While Oracle JSON-relational duality Views opens up new possibilities for developers, data modeling remains a critical success factor.

Index